LAWS AND LAWYERS IN TODAY'S AMERICA

THOUGHTS FROM THE INSIDE

MARK CLARK

WestBow Press®
A DIVISION OF THOMAS NELSON & ZONDERVAN

Copyright © 2016 Mark Steven Clark.

All rights reserved. No part of this book may be used or reproduced by any means, graphic, electronic, or mechanical, including photocopying, recording, taping or by any information storage retrieval system without the written permission of the author except in the case of brief quotations embodied in critical articles and reviews.

WestBow Press books may be ordered through booksellers or by contacting:

WestBow Press
A Division of Thomas Nelson & Zondervan
1663 Liberty Drive
Bloomington, IN 47403
www.westbowpress.com
1 (866) 928-1240

Because of the dynamic nature of the Internet, any web addresses or links contained in this book may have changed since publication and may no longer be valid. The views expressed in this work are solely those of the author and do not necessarily reflect the views of the publisher, and the publisher hereby disclaims any responsibility for them.

Any people depicted in stock imagery provided by Thinkstock are models, and such images are being used for illustrative purposes only. Certain stock imagery © Thinkstock.

ISBN: 978-1-5127-4219-0 (sc)
ISBN: 978-1-5127-4220-6 (hc)
ISBN: 978-1-5127-4218-3 (e)

Library of Congress Control Number: 2016907821

Print information available on the last page.

WestBow Press rev. date: 8/3/2016

This book is dedicated to my parents, Bob and Carol Clark, who recognized my lawyerly inclinations before I knew the meaning of the word. As they look down upon me, I hope they are as proud today as on the day that I graduated from law school.

This prayer is offered because justice is the touchstone of our Judeo-Christian ethic which enabled the colonies, and then the states, to create the most perfect nation the world has ever known.

Hebrew Prayer For Justice: Birkat HaMishpat

Restore our judges as in former times,
and our counselors as at first.
Remove us from sorrow and sighing,
and reign over us,
You alone, Adonai, with kindness and compassion,
with righteousness and justice.
Blessed are you, TRUE JUDGE,
who loves righteousness and justice.

Ancient prayer attributed to Rabbi Yohanan ha-Kohen (9th century)

TABLE OF CONTENTS

Preface xi
Chapter 1: Judges are Just Government Employees.......................... 1
Chapter 2: Just The Bad and The Ugly 7
Chapter 3: America: A Christian Nation 16
Chapter 4: The Hidden Conflicts 23
Chapter 5: The Unholy Alliance of Bar Associations and Courts. 34
Chapter 6: Lawyers – Behind the Scenes in A Law Firm 44
Chapter 7: (In)Famous Lawyers vs. the Legal System 48
Chapter 8: Why Do Attorneys Have Such A Bad Reputation?.......... 59
Chapter 9: The Bill Of Rights.. 65
Chapter 10: Interesting, Strange…and True!...................................... 90
Chapter 11: Secession, Nullification, and the Dept. of "Justice"........ 104
Chapter 12: "National Secrets and the 2&7/8 Government" 117
About the Author 131
Afterword.. 133
The Best True Lawyer Story Of All Time 135
Acknowledgments and Credits 137
Recommended Reading 139

PREFACE

*"When you wake up in the morning, tell yourself:
The people I deal with today will be meddling,
ungrateful, arrogant, dishonest, jealous and surly."*
                    Marcus Aurelius, Roman Emperor

When I began this book, I had no idea how overwhelming it would be. What started as a memoir, basically a collection of stories of cases in which I was involved or of which I had first-hand knowledge, started to morph into a different approach. Jack Skala was the person who put that thought into my head when he referred to the first three chapters as 'sour grapes'. Others who reviewed those chapters for me loved them and were anxious to see more. But Jack was right: the book lacked a necessary cohesiveness. It lacked a message. So I rethought my approach, and decided to write a critique of several sectors of the legal system, using not only my cases, but also those which I knew about, and many others that I researched. And then the book began evolving into a living history. Suddenly, there were new stories on a daily basis that bolstered my arguments: more lawyers indicted for crimes, more judicial corruption, more law enforcement corruption, more politically correct actions, etc. I began to think that I would never finish the book because the legal system kept providing so much information about its own flaws, and I could not keep up. Writing a history book must be easy by comparison. This book was taking on a life of its own.

We will discuss judges, lawyers, legal fees, conflicts of interest, America's Christian heritage, bar associations, the Bill of Rights, secession of the states, jury nullification, government power and corruption, and more. As you read the book its message will reveal itself to you: Do everything you can to avoid becoming entangled in the legal system. The timeworn adage of *"I'll see you in Court!"* is the worst possible means to resolve a dispute, and should be viewed as a last resort. But it's now often the first resort. America has more lawyers than any other nation on earth. We are a lawsuit driven society. This book will dissect the various parts of our system and the cast of characters that make it what it is. True case examples illustrate how the legal system really functions. When I offer an opinion, it is mine alone, based upon decades of experience and study. And being my opinion, and being the author, I have the prerogative to opine as I believe. You must draw your own conclusions. There is no fiction and nothing is minimized or exaggerated. The legal system seems to bend reality all by itself.

The law consists of statutes and regulations passed by Congress, state legislatures, and lesser branches of government, as well as case law (a written court opinion in a single case; the higher the court, the more important the opinion) that interprets the statutes and regulations. I was recently asked if I was going to write about our system of justice. I replied that America does not have a system of justice. America has a system of laws, whose goal is not justice, but rather social order. Our system of laws, regardless of their source, is intended to show people the consequences of their actions. But a justice system with justice as its purpose? No. When the law produces justice, it is a happy and often unexpected result. Nothing more nor less.

I am a retired lawyer. I began law school in 1973 and stopped all legal work decades later. The ensuing years have, on and off, been spent studying and researching this book. Those years have given me a unique perspective – I was an insider, now on the outside and looking back in. This is a unique pedestal from which I can discuss the legal system without fear of repercussions. Few lawyers have that privilege. I am unabashed in both my criticism and my praise. Recent surveys indicate that increasing numbers of lawyers around the country are coming to share my opinions and their own disenchantment with the system.

As I stand back and look at the system with an outsider's eye and an insider's knowledge, I become more and more concerned. It is not a question of winning or losing a case. It is a question of how the legal system affects peoples' lives. I am increasingly uncomfortable with my role in that system and often wonder how I affected the scale of justice. I pray for a positive balance, yet wonder whether the opposite is true.

This book is interesting. It is compelling. And it is all true. This book will not make me a hero in the legal profession; in fact, I may become more of a pariah. But that means I will have hit a lot of raw nerves by exposing the pieces of the systemic failure and explaining it to an interested and already jaded public. And that will be as gratifying as any profits from the book. Of course, you should still buy the book.

Lawyers write the laws. Sometimes, lawyers even know the law. Lawyers argue the law. Government lawyers regulate and police both the lawyers and the system. And everyone else? They are the grist for the mill that allows the system to churn and remain lucrative. As with any living organism, it must feed or it will die. You are its nutrition. It is a system of laws; not of justice.

With gratitude to Pat Conroy's remarkable <u>The Prince of Tides</u>, as I continue to cross the bridge from my life inside to the other side, I say these words with knowledge and trepidation. I say these words with respect and disdain. I say "Stay away. Stay away."

CHAPTER ONE

Judges are Just Government Employees

America has a problem that it cannot solve. All countries do. You see, our legal system is very political, and we cannot find a way to remove politics from the manner in which our judges are chosen. This is a problem that never occurred to our founding fathers because it had never arisen in the American colonies. The King chose the judges, the laws, and the government employees. But knowing no other system, our founding fathers did their best.

When the Constitution was written and the powers and duties of our 'checks and balances' three part government were defined, the only reference to selection of federal judges was that the President would nominate, "with the advice and consent of the Senate", the Chief Justice of the Supreme Court, and such other judges as may become necessary. The Senate has the right of confirmation. We have all seen the effects of this process. Judges nominated for seats on the U.S. District Court (the federal trial court) are rarely controversial or newsworthy. They are trial judges, with two layers of appellate courts above them. They are the work horses of the federal judiciary. They do the hard work but we cannot affect their choice by the president. After all, if they are federal judges, a lofty position in the system, then they must be honorable, wise, just, and above all else, knowledgeable in the law. Right? Not always. In the next chapter, I will show you some examples of inept, arrogant, and even harmful judges. The next level in the federal system is the appellate judges, followed by the justices of the Supreme Court. Their approval hearings by the Senate, are intensely focused on their prior rulings, clients, personal beliefs, conflicts of interest and loyalties. The smartest and most honest nominees are those who refuse to answer incendiary questions, citing the very legitimate grounds that they will not discuss matters upon which they will likely be called to render a decision. Ever since <u>Roe vs. Wade</u>, the primary issue has been abortion. It dominates Senate hearings and is often the sole issue that decides who our next appellate and Supreme Court justices will be. Although there are only one hundred people (101 if the vice-president has to be the tie-breaker) who decide to accept or reject these nominees, the process remains completely interwoven and dominated by the politics of the party that currently enjoys the senate majority. Consider how those people were nominated in the first place. Would the president nominate a person whose views are contrary to his? They do not. And the senators know, for the sake of their own careers, to vote the party line, often without regard to their personal beliefs. The selection system is inherently political. In the state and local courts, the problem is worse. Judges are either elected in the same way as other elected officials or the governor appoints them. Let's see what happens.

Elected judges are politicians first. They are on the ballot on Election Day to win the judgeship as members of one of the two dominant political parties. They have challengers. As campaigners for office they need money. Money comes from contributors, both large and small. Successfully elected judges, being as human as you and me, are susceptible to bias in favor of their contributors and other party officials or organizations. Does anyone truly believe that during their campaigns, the incumbent judges remain focused solely on their judicial duties? (If so, I have some bridges and water front property for sale…..). The alternative is for state judges to be appointed by the governor, often with the *'advice and consent'* of a screening committee. This is considered to be a merit selection system. These appointed judges are covert politicians. They often spend their early legal careers being active in their political party, collecting good will and political capital that will be repaid. Or they are active in their local and state bar associations, serving as committee members, officers, directors and cheerleaders for the 'public good'. In either event, they are politically active, and hope to earn their appointment as a reward for being a faithful party functionary *and for not rocking the boat*. Often, these judges are subject to a future binding or non-binding ballot question as to whether the voters believe they are doing a good job. For example, in Illinois an unfavorable vote is binding and removes the judge. In other states, such as Arizona, the voters' opinion is advisory and non-binding. I can recall only one instance when the voters expressed disapproval of a judge. Public opinion did not remove him from the bench, but did motivate the presiding judge to assign him to a less serious caseload. He resigned shortly thereafter.

Former U. S. Supreme Court Justice Sandra Day O'Connor, the first woman to serve on the Supreme Court, has expressed precisely the same opinion: We cannot protect our judicial system, and ensure that the law is applied fairly to everyone, until we can find a way to remove politics from the process of selecting judges. She posited the same problem and gave her own examples. There is nothing new about my opinion or hers; we simply agree, as do many other people. But the problem remains and no solution is in sight.

She argues in favor of merit selection, which I discussed on the prior page, but that system cannot work for the same reasons: the chosen judges are covert politicians. I agree that it is better than having our judges engage in partisan elections, but it does not ensure a better quality of judge or inspire greater confidence in the judicial system.

The state of Arizona has constitutionalized the best system yet to select judges. People are encouraged to apply for vacant judicial seats. A panel of lawyers and other people review the applications and choose whom to interview. After the interviews are concluded, the panel submits a list of three names to the Governor, who must select one of those three people. Now here is where the system is an improvement: Of the three people on the final list, no more than two can be in the same political party. One must be from the other party. And though it is counter-intuitive, sometimes the governor actually selects that third person based upon merit rather than political affiliation. That is a good start, which other states would be well advised to emulate.

But it is difficult to imagine any screening committee that is successful in its goal of independent recommendations. There are inherent political affiliations and favors owed and paid to applicants. The idea is good; the results are political. To believe anything else is naïve.

Please don't misunderstand me. There are many people who turn out to be competent or excellent judges, but there are also many who are wholly unqualified and prove to be incompetent. Because we have not removed politics from judicial appointments the problem continues unabated. Many of these 'bad' judges do not know the law, allow perjured testimony, allow lawyers who knowingly permit their witness or client to commit perjury (called 'suborning' perjury'), approve the use of improper evidence, and sometimes demonstrate a clear prejudice in favor of or against a particular lawyer or party by the judge's statements and body language. Jurors do not miss these cues. Roy Cohn, the attorney who represented Joseph McCarthy during his congressional witch-hunt in the 1950's, and who went on to a long and successful career, is reported to have said ***"I don't care if my opponent knows the law as long as I know the judge"***.

Who usually seeks out judgeships? One group is the lawyers who are unable, regardless of the reason, to succeed in their private law practice. For them, being a government employee brings a regular paycheck, employment benefits, a pension, banker's hours and prestige. Being a judge provides them security, which is their paramount goal. The second group is comprised of veteran prosecutors, many of whom are quite skilled and well-respected trial lawyers. But they have spent most or all of their careers working as prosecutors. When they become judges, try though they may, it is not possible to entirely remove their acquired bias in favor of the government and against the individual, regardless of whether it is a civil or criminal case. The minority of judges are lawyers seasoned in private practice who simply want to be a judge. But that can backfire as well. I recall an instance in Massachusetts many years ago, when one of the state's most respected superior court judges, whom everyone respected and believed would move up through the judicial hierarchy, suddenly announced his resignation and returned to private law practice. His reason? He was not paid enough as a judge to educate his children in the manner that he and his wife chose. He left the bench, by personal choice, so that he could better provide for his family. Wouldn't it make more sense to keep the 'best and the brightest' on the bench by paying them salaries commensurate with their duties and with the amount they can earn in a law firm? But few, if any, judges would have the audacity to publicly suggest that they be paid what they can earn in the private practice of law. The public and political outcry would make a pariah of such a judge.

The inescapable fact remains: the majority of state and local judges are either unsuccessful as lawyers or have spent their careers as government employees. Most successful lawyers in private practice either cannot afford to lose their income or choose not to do so. However, a minority of judges have sought the office because they are capable, and truly want, to impose the law in a just manner. If only they all had that ability and goal.

In his book <u>Letters to a Young Lawyer</u>, Alan Dershowitz wrote a fascinating review of some of the Supreme Court judges that he has watched or studied. Mr. Dershowitz, a professor at Harvard Law School, is one of America's preeminent legal minds and constitutional scholars. He has appeared in numerous high profile trials, appeals before the Supreme Court, and has taught at Harvard Law School for many years. He now receives dozens of requests per week for his services, but he only accepts cases that involve a novel legal issue, or cases in which it is apparent that a serious injustice may be developing. Of the cases that he does accept, he often works without pay, paying for his research staff, trial staff, travel and expenses out of his own pocket. (Another great American lawyer, Jerry Spence, does the same).

Mr. Dershowitz writes critically about some of the Supreme Court's most renowned jurists, such as Oliver Wendell Holmes, Felix Frankfurter, Hugo Black, and Williams O. Douglas. Louis Brandeis, Thurgood Marshall and Earl Warren also figure prominently in his criticism Yet their personal failures as human beings paled in comparison to the legacy that they left as Justices.

None of our judges, at any level, has ever been perfect, but we are entitled to a judiciary that is not biased, petty, or unethical. The judges pledge to 'administer justice without regard to people', but neither our judges nor our legal system have come close to achieving that goal. The legal system is deeply flawed in its application. The judges because, as are all people, they are products of their life experiences. That human flaw permeates every level of the judiciary.

CHAPTER TWO

Just The Bad and The Ugly

Let me give you some examples of bad judges and bad decisions. These examples come from federal courts, administrative courts, and state courts. No court at any level is exempt from the incompetence described in the next several pages.

I sat in a southwestern courtroom and watched the following scenario unfold. A mother and daughter were before a male Hispanic judge (now thankfully retired) seeking the renewal of a restraining order against the husband and father. The husband was extremely abusive, having subjected members of his family to physical, mental, emotional, financial and sexual abuse for sixteen years. After she finally escaped, the wife obtained her first restraining order to protect herself and her two minor children. For five years, the judges before whom she appeared had routinely renewed the restraining order (which her ex-husband routinely violated in an attempt to lure her back). At this particular hearing, the daughter had just turned 18, so being a legal adult, she needed her own restraining order. She was well aware of her father's plans for her, having watched him do it to her mother and to her *'au-pair'*. The mother and daughter both sought protection from the Court, and wrote substantially the same facts in each of their petitions for protection.

The Court hearing went like this (their names have been changed; the legal system has made them suffer enough), and I am paraphrasing to the best of my memory.

> **Judge:** *"Mrs. Smith, you want to renew your restraining order against Mr. Smith. Is everything in your affidavit true?"*
>
> **Mrs. Smith:** *"Yes, your Honor."*
>
> **Judge:** *"Do you have anything else you would like to add?"*
>
> **Mrs. Smith:** *"No, your Honor."*
>
> **Judge:** *"In that event, I see no reason not to renew this order for another year. And Mr. Smith, because you are present in the courtroom, consider yourself to be aware of this order now, although it will still be served upon you by a process server."*

Now it was the daughter's turn. She was just 18 and was quite nervous because her father was present *and* she had never been in a courtroom to speak publicly. Her hearing went like this.

> **Judge:** *"Ms. Smith, is everything in your affidavit true?"*
>
> **Ms. Smith:** *"Yes, your Honor",* having taken her cue from how the judge questioned her mother.

Judge: *"Do you have anything else you would like to add?"*

Ms. Smith: *"No, your honor."* (same cue)

Judge: *"In that event, since you have no facts to support your position, your request is denied."*

The daughter began to sob, feeling betrayed by the court that she believed would protect her from the father who had already betrayed her. Her shock and fear were legitimate. The court did betray her. And her father continued to pursue her.

At that point, the judge declared the hearings to be over and began to leave. I stood and asked if I might ask a question. He replied *"No"*. When I stated that he was publicly accountable and had just applied a double standard, he simply turned and walked away. No reply. No surprise, either.

Within months, having been pursued by her father with the Court's blessing, the daughter moved across the country to go to college. She has since stayed on the east coast and is unlikely to return to her home while her father is alive. Neither justice nor the law was served on that day. Instead, distrust and fear are a permanent part of her life.

But that judge did not stop his bizarre (and publicly reported) decisions. He sentenced a man who helped his friend shoot the friend's dog to thirty (30) days in jail, three years of probation, $1,846.00 in fines, and required that he attend animal cruelty prevention classes. Soon afterward, he sentenced a man *who killed another man by beating him to death, on the ground, by <u>repeated</u> blows with a rock* (in most states this would be deemed 1st degree murder) to only five years in jail. Five years! Perhaps my own morality is askew, but it seems that a human life is incomparably more important than a dog's life, and those two verdicts, from the same judge, in the same month, when contrasted against each other are simply not an understandable application of either the law or of common sense.

Since that time, there have been a few other cases, publicly reported, in which the same judge gave relatively light sentences to people that have been responsible for, or participated in, the death of other people. Not dog killers; people who have caused the death of other people. Even in the old west of the late 1800's, murder was a hangin' offense. Not anymore.

One year after the mother/daughter debacle, I received a summons for jury duty. About 400 jurors were summoned that day to fill out a lengthy questionnaire, which the same judge played a substantial role in preparing, for a first-degree murder trial (ironically, another sexually abused woman). The judge, prosecutor and defense lawyer reviewed all of the questionnaires, and rejected jurors that were clearly not acceptable. Despite my written answers on the lack of veracity of prosecutors and police officers, I was called back for jury selection. I have no idea why.

A strange set of events ensued. I was randomly chosen to be in the first group of jurors to go to the courtroom for further questioning. And then I was one of the first 14 jurors to be seated in the jury box for personal questioning by the judge and the lawyers. When the judge asked if anyone had any legal experience, I explained my background. After the judge finished with his questions, he turned to the prosecutor and said, *"I imagine that you would like to begin by talking with Mr. Clark"*. The prosecutor eagerly agreed and proceeded to grill me about my opinions of prosecutors and policemen. When asked if I believed that policemen would lie to obtain a conviction, and if prosecutors would knowingly allow that perjured testimony, I agreed and told her that I had seen it happen. The prosecutor sat down with a smug look of self-satisfaction: she had shown that I could not be fair. I then said to her, *"You did not ask the right question, so you only got part of the answer."* Taking the bait, she asked what I meant. I replied that when the questionnaire was prepared, the better question would have been, *"Do you believe that defendants, their witnesses, and the defense lawyers are as likely to commit and suborn perjury in order to win their case as prosecutors, victims, and their police officers?"* When she asked for my answer to the better question, I told her that I knew the defense was as likely to be dishonest as the prosecution, both seeking to obtain their version of *'justice'*. Needless to say, I was not picked to serve on the jury, but I believe that I showed the other potential jurors to be wary of both sides. The prosecution and the defense each seek *'justice'* in their own way, and knowing first-hand of that judge's erratic behavior, they needed that *'heads up'* for the defendant to have any chance at a fair trial.

Let's talk about other examples of incompetent judges, and the decisions and folly for which they earned that distinction. Please bear in mind that I am expressing my opinion about these judges, but the facts are all true.

In the mid 1970's, a wealthy black judge sat in a very poor inner city courtroom. I was in his courtroom 2-3 days per week as a third year law student, seeking appointments to represent indigent defendants (now a common and commendable program involving the courts and the law schools). I watched him routinely treat black defendants more harshly and with more disdain than he did with defendants of other ethnicities. There was no logical explanation for this insidious and odd form of discrimination, but every lawyer in the courtroom knew he was doing it. We will never know the reason, but he was the most consistently prejudiced judge that I have ever watched. And against his own race. But at least he was consistent. And if consistency is a virtue, he had at least that one.

In 2008, the mortgage and real estate bubble finally burst. Mortgage companies stopped writing high-risk mortgages because their investors would not buy them. People with adjustable rate mortgages suddenly found their monthly payments skyrocketing as their house values plummeted. Many Americans now owed more than their houses were worth. A large national lender filed for bankruptcy protection. That mortgage company laid off several thousand employee with no advance notice and no final paychecks. Many of those people, like so many Americans, lived from paycheck to paycheck. At the first hearing on the case, the company asked the judge to allow it to issue those final paychecks to its employees. At least the company sought to do the right thing. But the judge responded, *"Why do we need to pay any of these people? I understand the humanitarian reasons…..but shouldn't they just file claims and let it sort itself out?"* No, Judge, No! As you sit on the bench with a lifetime appointment, a six-figure salary and generous government benefits, these were normal working people who need to pay for housing, buy food, pay for utilities and car loans, health care, and their other living expenses. If you think you understand the '*humanitarian reasons*', you are living and judging in a society that you do not comprehend. On that day, your callous attitude towards those people hurt thousands of families and individuals and caused incalculable amounts of harm.

Two years later, the judge allowed the employees to receive their paychecks. Well, some of the employees. And only some of their money. The money certainly helped, but the large majority was not paid anything. And remember, at the very beginning the company asked permission to pay all of its employees their wages and salaries. Certainly the company had the cash to do so then, so what happened to that available cash? In a subsequent hearing, the judge approved pay *raises* for some of the company's remaining executives.

Here's an even better (or worse) one. A federal administrative law judge for the Social Security Administration, after a brief hearing, denied a claim for disability benefits for a person who suffered from acute depression, which in its worst forms is utterly debilitating, and who also suffered from chronic cardiac failure. The claimant provided affidavits from three board certified physicians, all in different specialties, attesting to his total disability. He included thirty-six monthly statements from his one physician confirming that he was totally disabled, could not work at all, and would remain so permanently. He provided notarized statements from five private citizens, all of whom knew him in different ways, attesting to his prior abilities and work standards, and the extent to which that changed when his health deteriorated so quickly. In addition, a neuropsychologist hired by Social Security agreed that the claimant was disabled, and Social Security's own occupational specialist testified that there was no gainful employment available in the American economy which he could reliably do on a regular, day in and day out, basis. All of the requirements and standards for disability benefits were met.

But not to be confused by the facts, Social Security hired two outside psychologists, neither of whom ever met, spoke with, or examined the claimant, nor did they ever talk to his physicians, attorney, or any witnesses. Nor did they appear in court to be cross-examined. Yet they wrote reports stating that they believed the claim was not valid and that the claimant was not disabled. They ignored all of the first-hand evidence, the affidavits of physicians, and even the testimony of Social Security's occupational expert. The judge used those second-hand hearsay reports to deny the claim, while ignoring all of the first-hand knowledge in front of him. He clearly does not understand the nature of chronic acute depression, nor of chronic cardiac failure, and should therefore not be ruling on medical issues about which he has no knowledge. His decision to even hear the case was inappropriate (it should have been approved administratively without a hearing), but he is paid by Social Security, and several of its employees have told me that SSA's goal is to weed out claims by taking years to assess them and bring them to court. It is denial by frustration.

That ruling, coupled by what I have learned from Social Security employees, confirms many peoples' belief that the real *'marching orders'* in the system are to deny claims, valid or not, in the knowledge that many claimants will be discouraged and drop their claim. It is normal for the Social Security Administration and its own judges to succeed in that endeavor. And for this treatment, those people have worked for years, paying FICA and social security taxes for exactly the insurance which their government actively seeks to deny them.

The claimant appealed to the Social Security Appeals Council in Washington, the *'highest court'* in the Social Security Administration. The Appeals Council sent the case back to the trial judge for a new hearing with a written opinion that left no doubt that he had completely mishandled the case. Specifically, he was ordered to consider the first hand evidence, and to document, by specific references to the evidence, the conclusions that he reached. In essence, the Appeals Council took him behind the wood shed and gave him a good whippin'. He took another year after the order from the Appeals Council to schedule the second hearing.

When he opened the second hearing, his audacity reached the point of a direct threat to the disability claimant. He stated that since the case was before him, he could re-examine and reconsider ALL of the prior action in the case, which by now included administrative approval of part of the claimant's claim of disability. In essence, he implied to the claimant that he could either drop his demand for a new hearing on the remaining disability claim (at which the judge might retroactively take everything away), or that he could continue with the hearing. Had the claimant agreed to drop the second hearing, the judge would not have had to embarrass himself by admitting that he had so grossly mishandled the first hearing. In as polite legal language as could be found, the judge was told to, well, perform an impossible act upon himself and that the hearing would continue. It did, and several months later, he ruled in favor of the claimant on all grounds. The entire process, from the application to the payment of benefits, took *six* years.

And let us never forget that Bill Clinton, while the sitting President, had his law license suspended for five (5) years by the Arkansas Supreme Court for having committed perjury against Congress about his gubernatorial extra-curricular activities. And it has been suggested, with good reason, that Hillary Clinton, the distraught wife and First Lady, might have been disbarred in Arkansas for her activities in the Rose Law Firm, the Whitewater debacle, 'missing billing records' scandal, and other matters, but for the fact that when testifying before Congress, she suffered severe amnesia and responded to most questions with *"I don't know"* or *"I can't remember"*. But she went on to become a serious presidential candidate and Secretary of State. Is there nothing that a dishonest lawyer or incompetent judge cannot accomplish? Kudos to whoever said that any American child can become President. It's true.

CHAPTER THREE

America: A Christian Nation

America is a Christian nation. America has always been a Christian nation. America is the greatest Christian nation that has ever been. For that, I am profoundly grateful. I was raised in a traditional Methodist congregation in the midwest at a time when there was no effort by anyone to shame Christians because of their faith. After a period in my adult life when I explored my Jewish ancestry and traditions, I returned to my Christian faith both renewed and comforted. As a friend recently suggested, I am a "Sermon on the Mount" Christian.

To say that America is a Christian nation is not to diminish America's greatness in another way. We are also the most tolerant nation ever to exist in regard to the right of any person to practice any religious faith, or if they choose, to practice no faith at all. Our tolerance flows from, and is a credit to, the people that founded America.

The European History

Christian persecution and violence against other Christians, which was commonplace in Europe for centuries, is a tragic and regrettable chapter in Christianity's long history. Nevertheless, it happened, and it would be revisionist history to deny the truth. More importantly for an understanding of America's genesis, it was the sole reason that many, often disparate, Christian groups fled Europe and came to this fledgling country. It was here that a new nation dedicated to religious freedom began.

Between 1620 and the 1776, when the Revolutionary War began, most of the people who emigrated from Europe to the American colonies did so because of religious persecution in their own countries. They were persecuted because their communities, and often their governments, denied them the right to worship as they chose. Protestants and Catholics alike insisted that uniformity of religion must exist in society and, of course, that their particular manner of worship was the only correct way to worship. The debate raged not over Jesus Christ, nor over God, but over the right way to worship both Christ and God.

Dutch Mennonites, or Anabaptists, were persecuted by Catholic authorities in Ghent. Jesuits such as John Ogilvie were under constant threats, and death, by the Protestant governments of England and Scotland. The Catholic ruler of Salzburg, Archbishop Firmian, expelled as many as 20,000 Lutherans from his principality. The Huegenots, or French Protestants, were slaughtered by Catholics at the start of thirty years of persecution and strife. Not to be out done, the Huguenots retaliated against the French Catholics with atrocities as harsh as that visited upon them. At the start of the Irish rebellion, in County Armagh, Irish Catholics murdered over one hundred Protestants by throwing them from a bridge. Those that did not drown were shot. John Rogers, a Catholic priest who converted to Protestantism, was the first Protestant martyr executed by the Catholic Queen Mary in England. In addition to Catholics persecuting Protestants and vice versa, many Jews fled northern and Mediterranean Europe to escape persecution by both Christians and Muslims.

Of those who crossed the Atlantic Ocean to escape religious persecution in Europe, and to a lesser extent, elsewhere, one of the largest groups was the Puritans. They were English Protestants, who wished to reform, or 'purify', the Church of England from what they considered the residues and influences of Roman Catholicism. Numbering as many as 20,000 people, they settled primarily in New England, where they established themselves in a religious community that they considered to be the true form of the Church of England. Of course, their expectation that the Church of England would see the errors of its ways would never come to pass. Jews largely settled in the port cities of Newport, RI, New York City, and Charleston, SC. Quakers, considered to be radical Puritans, adopted an ideology of austerity and 'plainness' and largely settled in Rhode Island and eventually, Pennsylvania, where their communities remain intact today. The Germans, who were largely Lutherans, settled in Pennsylvania. Roman Catholics gravitated to Maryland. In the largest colony, Virginia, the Church of England was recognized as the proper religion, and the colonial laws made the colony a bastion of Anglicanism. Taxes were collected by the local parishes to administer the obligations of local government, such as road repair and relief for the poor.

Thus, most of America's colonists arrived with the desire for religious freedom but often found that their predecessors had already established the 'correct' religion. Although persecution in colonial America never approached the horrors of Europe, many religious communities were intolerant of those who did not accept their way of believing.

Our Secular Government

To say that America is a Christian nation is in no way a denial of our secular form of government. Our federal government is comprised of three separate and co-equal branches: executive, legislative and judicial. They are meant to be free of religious influence and to function independently of one another. Their purpose is law. For the executive, it is to enforce the laws. For the legislative, it is to make the laws. And for the judicial, it is to interpret the laws. It is but a dispiriting commentary on modern politics that the lines between the three branches have become so blurred. Yet for each, their purpose is secular law. To allow any religious theocracy to obtain control of any of the branches of government would be a mockery of the Constitution and of the purpose of our form of government. Governments should be secular. Governments founded upon religion will always discriminate and persecute.

America Emerges

There is a more interesting question, which is this: After the Revolutionary War, when America was founded, was it established as a Christian nation? The answer to that question is found not only in the diversity of the colonists' experiences and diversity of faiths, but also in the language of the First Amendment to the U.S. Constitution. In the Establishment Clause and the Free Exercise Clause, these words are written: *"Congress shall make no law respecting an establishment of religion, or prohibiting the free exercise thereof."* What does this mean? It means that an official state, or government sanctioned, religion is forbidden in America. It also means that no person shall be denied their right to worship as they choose. All Americans were thus free to worship, or abstain from worship, as their conscience required. And no person could be forced to adhere to a religion approved or mandated by the government. Although the 1st Amendment in its entirety was not expressly binding upon the states until 1867, all states had 'disestablished' religion by 1833. Massachusetts was the last. This ended the practice of allocating taxes to churches as well.

And thus, America became the first, and to this date, the greatest nation on earth both in regard to our tolerance for the observance of all religions and also the great Christian virtue of kindness. We are the greatest Christian nation to emerge in 2,000 years.

It was not long before this question was put to the test in the international arena. In the 1790's, Muslim pirates began raiding American and European shipping along the Barbary Coast, which is the northwestern horn of Africa. In 1797, President John Adams negotiated a peace treaty with the Barbary pirates, which was ratified by a unanimous U. S. Senate.

The peace treaty was a commonplace diplomatic solution, but has earned its place in history because of language that was inserted in its text. The treaty stated that the United States was *"Not, in any sense, founded on the Christian religion."* This language was meant to appease the Muslim fear that the United States would interpret the treaty under Christian terms. (A fear I cannot comprehend.) But by including that language, perhaps because we were a young and untested nation, the point was made that the treaty was a secular agreement between two nations and not between two religions. Many today see that language as America's first concession to Islam, but that is simply wrong. It was simply the affirmation of America's official status as a secular state and a reassurance to the world that America would operate in the international arena on the basis of secular, rather than religious, priorities.

After the establishment of America as an independent country, many religions proliferated over the following decades. The Church of England retained its influence and evolved into the Episcopalian Church. "Great Awakenings", or religious revivals, took place, and gave rise to the Methodist and Baptist churches, as well as the Holiness movement, the Nazarene movement, and the Christian Science church. Protestant evangelicalism gave rise to the African-American Christian faiths in Baptist and Methodist churches. Restorationism, Mormonism, Jehovah's Witnesses and the Christian Science Church all sprang from America's fundamentalist Christians, each seeking its own way to worship as Christians. And America gave birth to many other religious movements, such as the Seventh Day Adventists, the Church of Christ, the national Baptist Convention, Pentecostalism, Reform and Reconstructionist Judaism, Scientology, the Southern Baptist Convention, and Unitarian Universalism. Today, every religion in the world are freely practiced in America. And the free exercise of religious practices and beliefs is encouraged here more than anywhere else. It is because of America's Judeo-Christian heritage that we are the shining light in the world.

Religious Extremism

Given the current polarization of American society and politics, as well as international society and politics, this is an opportune time to discuss religious extremism. Let me say it plainly: religious extremism in any faith serves the God of no faith. Whether the extremism is Islamic vs. Christian, Islamic vs. Jewish, Hindu vs. Islamic, Christian vs, Jewish, or even atheism vs. any faith, the extremists are on the outside of their religion. They are pariahs in any society. Their fanatical acts serve only to polarize them from the beliefs and morality of any right thinking person.

Yet we see examples around us every day. Islamic terrorists slaughter Christians, Jews and even other Muslims. The hatred between Pakistan's Muslims and India's Hindus has not abated for almost a century. And in America, we see the hatred of the members of the Westboro Baptist church who protest primarily at funerals of American soldiers killed in action, the Tempe, Arizona pastor who publicly called for the execution of all homosexuals as a way to eradicate AIDS, the southern Baptist minister who publicly and proudly burned the Quran, the antisemitism and racial hatred of white supremacists, and, in our not so distant past, the racial hatred and terror perpetrated by the Ku Klux Klan while cloaking themselves in Christianity.

None of these individuals or groups is representative of their faith or honest emissaries of their God. Religious extremism is not limited to any one religion. It infects all religions and, like any disease, must be eradicated to ensure that all people throughout the world can freely and safely practice the religion of their choice

CHAPTER FOUR

The Hidden Conflicts

Only a few lawyers, and very few clients, understand that the very nature of their relationship, in addition to being privileged and sacrosanct, is the most insidious conflict of interest. Most lawyers do not understand, or acknowledge, this inherent conflict. It rears its ugly head in many ways: misunderstandings over legal fees, the extent of the lawyer's representation vs. the client's expectation, success or failure of the client's case, representing groups of people whose interests are often in conflict, the guilty defendant who insists on exercising his constitutional right to testify, which the lawyer condones, and so on. No one, certainly including myself, can ever foresee all of the potential conflicts between lawyer and client, but they are inherent in the relationship. They are normally a failure of communication, which is the lawyer's burden, or a deliberate or ignorant decision by the lawyer to accept a case in which a conflict is obvious and inescapable. As a result, the relationship often deteriorates, which leads to more lawyers, more lawsuits, more legal fees, ad infinitum. There are hundreds of jokes and stories about legal fees and I assure you that every one of them has happened at one time or another. They are not jokes. This should be an ongoing source of embarrassment to lawyers, but it is not. For the most part, they count their gold coins and plan for more. Clients are the means to their end. As for the inherent conflict over legal fees, I will discuss those in the second half of this chapter.

So let's talk about some of these 'invisible' conflicts that can cause the worst problems between lawyer and client. First, consider a criminal case. Almost everyone inside the system knows, and everyone outside of the system believes, that most people charged with crimes are guilty. Fact is, they are. So let's create a hypothetical situation: A new client, charged with murder, retains you to defend him. He tells you that he is guilty, or by some other means, you learn that he is guilty. It doesn't matter how you come by the knowledge; you know the truth. Your client insists on testifying in his own behalf, and you know that he will perjure himself by denying the crime. The lawyer cannot suborn the perjured testimony, but the defendant has an *absolute constitutional right to testify in his own behalf.* You, as his lawyer, are in a terrible quandary. You have agreed, and sworn upon your oath as an attorney, that you will zealously represent him to the best of your ability. So how should you handle the situation? A criminal defense lawyer first tries to persuade the client not to testify. Failing that, he seeks permission from the Court to resign as the defendant's lawyer. Failing that, he may contact the State Bar and seek their advice. Failing that, he may ask the judge for permission to withdraw from the case. And if all else fails, he will use leading questions with his client to try to work around and avoid the issue(s) about which his client intends to commit perjury. But many lawyers question the defendant as if nothing was amiss, and by doing so, commit a felony for which they should be imprisoned and disbarred. They have suborned perjury, which they then use in their closing argument. Many judges turn a blind eye, and the dishonest lawyer will always swear that he never knew the testimony was false. He cites the attorney-client privilege and refuses to discuss matters that he discussed with his client. And the real irony? The only person who can 'bust' the lawyer is his own client. How much worse can a conflict of interest be?

Now let's consider a hypothetical civil lawsuit. You, as the attorney, represent an injured plaintiff who is seeking damages (read: money) from the person or company that injured her. She has a good case, but it has some weaknesses, and you know that she could win or lose at trial. A settlement of $250,000.00 is offered to her. You believe it is a good offer, and advise her to accept it. She refuses, wanting a larger settlement or a jury award. You know a trial is throwing her fate to the wind. She loses control over the result and leaves her fate in the hands of strangers. You have a couple of conflicts with her now. First, you believe she is making a bad decision contrary to your advice. Second, you want your one-third (1/3) contingency fee from the offer, and know that if you lose at trial, you will be paid nothing. Furthermore, if you lose at trial, your client will be angry at you. She does not have the $250,000.00, she lost the case, and the obvious person who made the mistake is you. Otherwise, she would have won the trial. So guess who she sues next? If she can't get her money one way, she will get it in another. And whether you win or lose when she sues you, your malpractice insurance premiums will skyrocket, or your insurance may not be renewed next year.

The next situation involves conflicts between clients. An attorney cannot represent a client if his representation conflicts with information he learned from other clients, particularly if the adversary is a former client. Most medium and large law firms run a computer check looking for conflicts before the lawyer will even talk to the new client. Those lawyers and law firms that do not cross-check their possible conflicts and list of past and current clients run the risk of personal liability and ethical problems. Here's an example.

In 1997, I took a different state's bar exam. The second day of the exam consisted of ten hypothetical problems we were expected to resolve. We had six hours to answer the ten questions. One of our questions went like this (and I paraphrase): A wife and mother passed away, leaving her husband and adult son. They come to you and ask you to probate the estate. The situation looks simple enough and is well within most lawyers' ability. The mother left no will, but she owns the house jointly with her husband, she has her own 401(K) plan without a named beneficiary, she has a bank account for an inheritance she received from her parents, a joint bank account with her son, and she and her husband equally own all of their personal effects and joint investments, including joint bank accounts. There are also common debts, and she has some credit cards in her name alone. And their son owes money to his mother from her inheritance. As I read the question, the answer regarding distribution of her estate was obvious. But do you know that feeling when your intuition says that something is not right? Well, my intuition was screaming at me. The problem was too easy for a bar exam question. Finally, I realized that the question had nothing to do with probating the estate. It was about the inherent rights and claims of the husband and son, which are definitely in conflict. It does not matter whether they agree on the resolution of the estate. It only matters that there is a conflict of interest. The answer to the question? The lawyer cannot represent them together or either of them separately. In fact, having met with both of them, the lawyer cannot be involved in the estate at all. It was a subtle trick question, and I am willing to bet that most of the experienced lawyers, and virtually all of the new law school graduates, missed the real issue. Yet it happens in lawyers' offices all the time. Many lawyers will ignore the conflict in order to be paid to handle the estate. If problems do develop between husband and son, the lawyer may as well walk into a pool of quicksand, or call the state bar and confess. Ultimately, the risk and liability again fall on the lawyer.

Part 2 – Legal Fees

Legal fees create a conflict in *every* attorney-client relationship. There are several ways in which legal fees can be handled. Common sense says the fee agreement should always be written. It often is not. Each state defines what constitutes a 'reasonable' legal fee. The analysis involves time spent, the result achieved, the difficulty of the case, the lawyer's expertise in that area, whether the lawyer lost other work while handling the case, the urgency of the representation, and a few others. Let me define the various fee arrangements, each with their pros and cons, and give you some examples as we go along. I will also show you several ways in which many lawyers pad their bills without your knowledge.

1) <u>The Hourly Rate</u>. As its name says, a lawyer may take your case based upon a flat hourly rate, from which she expects two things: to pay her overhead and to earn a good living. As the client, you expect that each hour for which you are billed she will devote one hour solely to your case. I have seen hourly rates as low as $75.00 and as high as $1,000.00. Rates are occasionally higher for senior partners in major law firms. The rate will reflect the lawyer's skills, experience, and whether she is in Manhattan or Montana. Sometimes the $75.00 is appropriate; other times the $1,000.00 is appropriate. The decision is yours. She will ask for a retainer (advance payment) that she will hold in her trust account and draw out as she does the work. In addition, you are responsible for out of pocket expenses, such as court filing fees, depositions, and expert witnesses.

Furthermore, it is normal for lawyers to bill in increments of an hour: $1/4^{th}$, $1/6^{th}$, $1/10^{th}$. The worst example I have seen was a lawyer who billed in increments of $1/100^{th}$ of an hour. That is 36 seconds. I referred a client to him with a post-divorce problem. He wanted a $5,000.00 retainer. The client told him she could pay only $1,000.00 in advance, but she would promptly pay each monthly bill. He refused to take the case on that basis, but a few weeks later sent her a bill that included the first meeting, *as well as* unauthorized 'research' and 'consultations' with three lawyers <u>*after*</u> he refused the case. By no coincidence, the bill was approximately

$1,000.00, the amount he knew she had available. He wanted her money but not her case. By billing her for things he 'did' after refusing the case, I believe that his bill was outright fraud. Upon my insistence, she rightly refused to pay the bill. Perhaps knowing how inappropriate the bill was, he never pursued her for the money.

Ways that lawyers commonly pad their bills include an invoice that includes two lawyers in the firm talking about your case and then having both of them bill for their time. When this happens, it is common for the lawyers to charge for unequal amounts of time in the meeting, which means they are each increasing their billable hours without regard to accuracy or integrity, or without the elementary safeguard of agreeing on the time they spent together. Sometimes they even cite different reasons for the meeting. Even professional criminals plan their activities carefully, including their escape. Lawyers are not that smart; just more greedy. Another way is to charge for travel time, but you will never convince me that your lawyer is spending all of that travel time thinking only about your case. They are also working on someone else's case by phone or by thought. Because there is no way to prove this, they are billing two clients for the same time. There is the oft-quoted story of an attorney flying coast to coast in behalf of client A, but he spent the entire flight doing work on client B's case. Are you surprised that he charged them both for the time of the flight?

A few years ago, I had a corporate client in San Diego, who was being represented on a local matter by a local attorney. His hourly rate was $375.00. Fortunately my client's president ran a tight ship, and the president discovered, while reviewing one of the lawyer's monthly bills, that his company was being charged for thirty minutes, or $187.50, for travel time to attend a negotiating session. As I said before, it is not uncommon for lawyers to charge for travel time, and it is one of the traps for the unwary client, but this one was exceptionally greedy. Why? *The entire length of his '30-minute' trip was taking the elevator downstairs to a lower floor in the same building.* In a different audit, a Houston lawyer was found to have charged his client $165.00 for 'ground transportation' that turned out to be a new pair of shoes.

Here is another one that I was personally involved in (I was not the lawyer who sent this bill.) My client lost a civil jury case and hired an appellate specialist for the appeal. The appellate lawyer's hourly rate was $335.00, and his young associate's rate was $180.00, for a combined rate of $515.00 per hour. For the initial meeting with their new client, they drove together from Phoenix to Tucson, spent 6 hours with the client, and returned to Phoenix. There were two problems with that bill. First, they charged three hours to travel each direction when it only takes two hours, and second, the associate's presence, at $180.00 per hour, was not necessary. In sum, that meeting, just for the lawyers to meet the client and do an initial intake, cost the client over $6,000.00. The appellate lawyer never did prepare or argue the appeal and lost every post-trial hearing and motion that he filed and argued for the client. His total bill was in excess of $116,000.00, and it was upheld by an 'objective' fee arbitration panel chosen by the State Bar. Two of the three chosen arbitrators were lawyers, and the Bar also chose the one regular citizen. Having already received $115,000.00, he had the audacity to demand the remaining $1,000.00+, which he was awarded. That lawyer is now a federal judge.

And finally, although I cannot vouch for the truth of this story, the rumor in Boston in the late 1970's was that a prominent law firm charged one of their best clients $1,800.00 *to prepare his bill.* As it turns out, more and more large firms are charging to prepare bills. For centuries, the law has called itself an honorable profession. What sayeth thee?

2) <u>The Flat Fee</u>. In many cases, particularly when the lawyer has a good idea of how much time he will spend on a case, he will charge a flat, or fixed, fee. He will want it in advance and it is often non-refundable for any reason. Success or failure is not relevant to any adjustment of the fee. The problem with a flat fee is that if the lawyer has not completed your case, but has used all of the fee (based on his hourly rate and his usual 'add-ons'), he will start to lose interest in your case, feeling that he is now working for free. So procedures that need to be done, motions or briefs that need to be prepared, and trial preparation are often done as quickly as possible, with speed being more important than quality or integrity. And if the lawyer concludes your case in less time than anticipated, there will not be a voluntary refund of the excess. One egregious example that affected a family member was a $10,000 fee for two court appearances and an office meeting, a total of less than two hours.

3) <u>The Contingent Fee.</u> It is used almost exclusively in personal injury cases where someone has been injured and seeks monetary damages. The lawyer will take the case, and work it hard to maximize the settlement or judgment, and then charge a percentage of the money collected as his fee. If he loses, he receives no fee. The contingent fee can range from 20% to 50%. Some states cap it at 33%; 40% if there is an appeal. Others set no parameters, but anything in excess of 40% is clearly unreasonable. The lawyer commonly advances all of the out-of-pocket expenses, and recoups them as follows: When the money comes in, he first deducts his 33%, and then reimburses himself his expenses from your 67%. The only unforeseen trap is if your case is lost, you still reimburse the lawyer for the expenses.

One of my clients was owed $35,000.00 in commissions for insurance sales that she made. She left the insurance company before she was paid, and when she was gone, they refused to pay her. Having had previous dealings with the same insurance company, I had a conflict of interest, so I took her to my own lawyer and he agreed to take the case on a contingent fee of 33%. He wrote a letter to the president of the insurance company, who knew the saleswoman personally, demanding the money that she had earned. One week later, due to the president's intervention, the $35,000 was paid. All it took was one well-written letter and the initial consultation with her attorney. After discussing the fee issue with me, he agreed to accept $5,000.00. Her lawyer was satisfied; I was happy; and the client was irate, until we both explained to her the realities of a long lawsuit, which includes the possibility of losing, and that he could have demanded 33%. She finally agreed that I had done the right thing. So she paid $5,000.00 for less than two hours of work, and was satisfied. I agree. The fee was reasonable based upon the result. The only other rule is this: A lawyer can *never* use a contingency fee in a divorce or criminal case.

4) <u>The Menu Fees.</u> The use of the word 'menu' is my own; it is not a common term for fees. Here are some examples of how it works: You consult with an attorney about preparing wills for yourself and your spouse. This is easy work for the lawyer because the templates are already on his computer. But he will also take the opportunity, as he should, to explain trusts, durable powers of attorney, living wills, and health care powers of attorney. The law does not require you to have any of these documents but they are all important. So there is a 'menu' presented to you, and you choose which documents you do or do not want. The lawyer will then quote the fee based on what you have chosen.

Another example in which this works well: I have used the same arrangement when I created a corporation, limited liability company or partnership for my client. They may also want stock redemption agreements, employment contracts, vendor contracts, and so on. Again, the client picks and chooses what they want, and the lawyer charges accordingly. This procedure was most popular with my clients because they were in control of their legal fees. They tended to be the most satisfied clients, and were most likely to refer other people to me.

There are just two hard and fast rules regarding legal fees: the client is always responsible for out-of-pocket expenses. And the lawyer will almost always profit.

Other ways to pad your bill, and I have no doubt missed some, are:

charging for postage, photocopies, fax transmissions, dedicated 'thinking' about your case (beyond a reasonable amount of time), rent for office space, couriers, librarians, and even heating, ventilating and air conditioning (HVAC).

Many larger firms charge different rates for senior partners, junior partners, associate lawyers, paralegals and even secretaries. What to watch for besides all of the above? Charging the senior partner's rate for work done by a junior partner, charging the paralegal rate for work done by a secretary, etc. Another red flag on your bill is when the firm replaces one lawyer with another on your case. You should never pay for the second lawyer to get 'up to speed' on your case. It was the firm's decision to change lawyers so the firm should absorb the cost.

I think my favorite story about legal fees is the Illinois lawyer who was suspended from practicing for fifteen months because, as a part of his fee, he accepted nude dances in his office from his client – a stripper – as partial payment of his fee. He did credit her with $534 on her bill. Given that the U.S. Supreme Court has ruled that full or partial stripping, lap dances, and even hard-core pornography are expressions of free speech under the 1st Amendment, what did he do wrong? Is it because it was in his office? No, that can't be, because the right of free speech does not stop at a lawyer's office door. If anything, it is enhanced because of the attorney-client privilege. Is it because she was a stripper, and thus was scorned by the Illinois Bar Association? No that can't be, again due to the right of free speech. Did he fail to report the value of her services as income and pay taxes on it? If so, that only becomes a bar discipline issue if the IRS or the Illinois Dept. of Revenue has convicted him of criminal tax charges. Barter of services or goods is absolutely legal and taxable. In fact, 'couch' fees, in which the lawyer is paid with sex, are common in the profession. Although deemed ethically unacceptable, the entire transaction falls within the 1st Amendment. But there are lawyers and Bar Associations that absolutely condemn sex as payment, even if written into a fee agreement, and believe that disbarment should be automatic. Based on the 1st Amendment, I cannot agree.

So how do we explain that the client's exercise of free speech, to which the client and lawyer both consented, was grounds for bar discipline?

Make any sense? Not to me.

CHAPTER FIVE

The Unholy Alliance of Bar Associations and Courts.

There are two types of bar associations: integrated and non-integrated. This has nothing to do with segregation; it refers to the relationship between the state, the bar association and the lawyers. In a state where the bar is not integrated, membership in a Bar association is voluntary, and the role of the association is continuing education, lawyer referrals for the public, fee arbitration, etc. But you must still be licensed, which is approved by the state supreme court. And yes, there is always a separate organization, a 'board of bar overseers' with its own law firm, 'office of bar counsel'. Their sole function is the prosecution and discipline of lawyers.

In states that have an integrated bar, membership in the state bar is compulsory because the state bar is an arm of the state supreme court. Annual dues are paid directly to the bar, and the money is used to prosecute and discipline lawyers, as well as to monitor compulsory continuing education, and to 'work for the public good'. But the bottom line in both arrangements is there is a 'law firm', controlled by the state supreme court, which exists solely to prosecute lawyers. Its prosecutors tend to be arrogant, inflexible and self-righteous. Bar prosecutors will always tell you they are protecting the public. Hogwash! The public needs lawyer referrals, and access to pamphlets written in plain English that explain various types of legal services, including *"Do you need a lawyer?"* Every lawyer who receives a letter from the state bar feels his pulse quicken and blood pressure rise as he opens the envelope, never certain what to expect. Let there be no question, the success of this subcategory of lawyers is judged by how many lawyers they have successfully prosecuted each year. Sometimes they are right, but I am also going to give you an example where a lawyer was disciplined although the bar could not explain what rule he had violated, and another example where the bar punished a lawyer (me) for refusing to sign a fraudulent tax return. Do not believe that there is any more integrity from the bar's prosecutors than from the lawyers they prosecute, or the criminal defendants that a public prosecutor indicts and a defense lawyer defends.

Before addressing the specific cases, let me tell you some of the basic truths about lawyer prosecution. First, the purpose of bar prosecutors is to aid the state supreme courts to *control* lawyers. Why? Because the legal knowledge and skills that a lawyer has, although necessary in the legal system, gives the lawyers superior knowledge and ability, in both public and private matters, every hour of every day. In the system's eyes, lawyers must be controlled by the government. Left alone, lawyers are deemed 'rogues' in society, and that is a risk that the state and federal governments do not want to countenance. Second, they are far more likely to investigate and pursue sole practitioners and 2-3 lawyer firms than the large institutional firms. Why? The sole practitioners and small firms are competition that the large firms want to chase away. The 'little guys' usually charge less and get the work done faster. The perception is that they are taking business away from the large firms. And they are. Would you rather pay $1,000.00 or $5,000.00 for a full estate plan? The effect and content of the documents will be similar or identical. The only difference is the attitude and fee practices of the particular lawyer or law firm. So the bar protects the large firms and the political insiders and seeks to weed out the competition because it is the larger firms that a) are more likely to support the bar with donations, b) offer voluntary commitments from their firms to render free legal services and, c) work actively to maintain the present system from the challenges against it. The sole practitioners and small firms focus primarily on their work to support themselves and their office although many of them do pro-bono work voluntarily. And sometimes involuntarily (read: not being paid).

And finally, would you expect bar prosecutions to be as fair and open as normal courtroom proceedings? The answer should be *"Yes.",* but the truth is *"Absolutely not."* When the bar decides that a lawyer has acted improperly, it appoints the hearing officer who hears the case, and when you lose at the hearing (which you can expect), your appeal is to a disciplinary commission composed of bar appointed members, most of whom are hand-picked lawyers. They routinely uphold the hearing officer's decision. Your next avenue of appeal is to the state supreme court, which almost automatically follows the decision of the disciplinary commission. So when the bar decides to prosecute, they are the prosecutor, the judge and jury, and the appeals 'courts'. Nice arrangement for the government but lethal to the lawyers ensnared in it. A rattlesnake's bite has less venom. The bar associations and the courts both believe that they are the sole arbiters over lawyers. Their only problem is when the Constitution gets in their way. Lawyers argue every day about due process, equal protection, and objectivity for their clients. Yet they deny it to themselves. Now let's look at some real life examples. I think you will agree with me.

The public awareness of bar prosecutions began over twenty years ago in a well-publicized Illinois case. In that case, a lawyer who had nothing to do with a transaction that took place, was aware that one of the lawyers involved had mishandled money in the transaction. The uninvolved lawyer simply knew the facts. Nothing else. The Illinois Supreme Court suspended his license for six months because he did not immediately notify the bar of the other lawyer's conduct. He personally did nothing wrong.

Thus was born the 'rat rule'. Lawyers became personal adversaries against each other and two new specialties were born: lawyers suing lawyers and lawyers defending lawyers. Every lawyer in America shuddered when that case was decided by the Illinois Supreme Court, because we all knew that sooner or later, our states would adopt the 'rat rule'. And most states have. Lawyers have become their own worst enemies.

In Washington state, an unusual case came to the attention of the Bar prosecutors. Follow this closely; it's a little confusing. An attorney, who had since been appointed as a judge, was thrown off the bench when another attorney disclosed that he learned from a client that the now-judge had represented an estate and made a secret agreement to sell a bowling alley belonging to the estate at a price far below fair market value. At about the same time, the future judge received a new Cadillac from the buyer of the bowling alley. It was clearly an unethical act and a betrayal of his fiduciary duty as representative of the estate. Ten years later, the judge's conduct led to his removal from the bench and the suspension of his law license for two years.

Now the case took an unexpected turn. The bar prosecutors went after the lawyer who made the disclosure, ruling that he violated the attorney-client privilege by disclosing the information he learned from his own client. The Washington Supreme Court upheld the decision and his license was suspended for six months for disclosing the judge's prior conduct. In fairness, there was an exacerbating issue. The lawyer who made the disclosure waited seven years to do so, and he only did so after the corrupt judge had imposed a punishment against him for filing a frivolous lawsuit. What a conundrum for the Washington Supreme Court: The judge was clearly wrong and his punishment was, if anything, generously short, while the attorney's belated disclosure, after his reprimand from the judge, was clearly an act of vengeance against the judge. The Washington Supreme Court ruled that the attorney-client privilege was more important than the 'outing' of a corrupt judge, so the lawyer was suspended. So let's take this problem to its logical extreme.

What would you do, as an attorney, if you learned from your client that an innocent man was on death row and scheduled for execution? Which do you choose: violating the attorney-client privilege to save the man's life, or withholding the information to avoid violating the attorney-client privilege, while the innocent prisoner dies? How would the Washington Supreme Court handle that case?

Remarkably, this exact situation came to light in an Illinois case, reported in the media in April 2008. The only difference was a sentence of life in prison without parole rather than the death penalty. But an innocent man spent twenty-six years in prison while two lawyers, two public defenders knew the truth – he was innocent. But the attorney-client privilege kept them from revealing the truth, and the man who was guilty, and is now dead, was never charged with the crime. It went like this: A man named Alton Logan was convicted of murder for killing a security guard in a McDonald's restaurant in 1982. But another man, Andrew Wilson told his two public defenders that he, and not Logan, had killed the security guard. The lawyers, who at the time worked together as public defenders, had Wilson sign a notarized affidavit that he was the killer. But there was a catch: the attorney-client privilege. They knew an innocent man had been convicted of murder and was in prison for life. They consulted with legal scholars, ethics commissions and the Bar association. Each time they were told there was nothing they could do: the attorney-client privilege required them to remain silent. Finally, in January, 2008, with a court's permission, the lawyers revealed their secret in court. As a result, Logan got a new trial – not exoneration and a pardon – but only a new trial.

In a prison interview, Logan summed it up perfectly. He said,

"What I can't understand is you know the truth, you held the truth and you know the consequences of that not coming forward? Is a job more important than an individual's life?"

As much as I dislike and do not trust bar prosecutors with their self-righteous attitude, I concede that some of their cases are hard to call due to mitigating or exacerbating factors, or a conflict in the rules. As a justice on the Washington or Illinois Supreme Courts, how would *you* handle these predicaments?

Recently, an anti-war protest rally was held in Tucson by a radical yet non-violent women's group. The police had never had any problems at that group's public rallies or meetings. Yet the police put an undercover officer in the crowd. During the rally, an attorney, who was a member of the protest group, recognized the undercover police officer and revealed his identity to everyone present. The official reaction was draconian. The police department announced that it would no longer allow defense lawyers to interview undercover officers in person because the lawyers might reveal their identities. This hampers the defense lawyers who lose the ability to observe an officer's demeanor and assess their credibility before they testify against a defendant. It was a foolish knee-jerk reaction by the police department to warn lawyers that the police would take punitive measures against lawyers who did not follow 'their' rules. A bar complaint was filed against the lawyer who 'busted' the undercover officer, which the bar took seriously enough to investigate the incident. The lawyer was later determined to have done nothing wrong and the charges against her were dropped. What never made the press, and therefore the general public, was that the lawyer had a first amendment right of free speech, and she had done nothing to violate that. The whole ritual of indignation, anger and investigation was nothing more than a ruse to intimidate the public and other lawyers. The effort failed. To the chagrin of the bar, by being the supreme law of the land in regard to individual rights, the U.S. Constitution trumps state bar association rules. As a result, the lawyer won, and the relationship between the lawyers and the police deteriorated even more. And likely, the ability of defense lawyers to fully and vigorously represent their clients has been compromised – another constitutional problem.

Shortly afterward, the State Bar of Arizona proposed a rule requiring that the rules governing lawyer conduct be applicable twenty-four hours per day, seven days per week. A former president of the state bar responded with this hypothetical: There is a long-term rivalry between the University of Arizona and Arizona State University. Emotions run high. The former bar president is an ardent University of Arizona fan. So if she wears a tee shirt with an obscenity about the other team on it, she will certainly offend ASU fans. The bar wanted that to be an ethical violation and to require that lawyers *"avoid the appearance of impropriety"* and *"avoid conduct that would offend another person"* at all times. If the 24/7 rule was in effect, she would have committed an ethical violation in a football stadium on a Saturday afternoon while cheering for her team. Surprisingly, the bar realized that her constitutional right of free speech takes priority, and that the rule was unenforceable. But the chairman of the Professionalism Task Force that recommended the 24/7 rule is reported to have said there must be an effort to hold lawyers to a higher standard than anyone else because the existing ethical rules do not cover all the situations in which a lawyer might act unprofessionally. In the case of the tee shirt, he believes that wearing it would be unprofessional and should be grounds for discipline. Thus, lawyers who act 'unprofessionally' in their *private lives* would be subject to professional sanctions. And who decides what is inappropriate in their private lives? Yes, the government.

In one prosecutor's office, there is a senior prosecutor who is a self-proclaimed lesbian and is active in the gay rights cause. Her sexual orientation is public knowledge by her own choice. If you or I feel that her sexual choice is offensive, do you expect her to stop that private activity, or to switch teams and become heterosexual? Does she want her sexual orientation to be subject to the approval of the state bar? Would she comply with that rule in any event? So state bar, tell us how you would enforce that rule without tripping over the Bill of Rights. Again. It is time for the bar and the courts to sit down, cool off, regain their humility, and rethink their attitude towards lawyer conduct with full deference to the Constitution, particularly the 1st Amendment rights of free speech and free assembly and the 4th Amendment guarantee of equal protection. And, of course, the 14th Amendment, which imposes the Bill of Rights on state and local governments.

Early in my career, I found myself in a completely untenable position, in which I could do no right. If I obeyed the law, I was in ethical trouble. If I violated the law, I was safe. This ludicrous result was sanctioned by the bar association. It went like this: An existing client asked if I would probate her father's estate. I met with the family and agreed to accept the case. While going through his personal effects, the family found a safe deposit box key. Her father left no will so we obtained the necessary permission to access the safe deposit box. I went to the bank with her, and we discovered a large box completely filled with rare coins, silver dollars, collectors' mint sets of stamps and coins, and some cash. There were thousands of individual items, mostly loose coins. We began to inventory the box. She kept a list of each item. When the bank closed, and we had to leave, I told her to sign and date the list, and to verify that it was a partial list of the contents of the box. We made an appointment to meet at the bank again, which she canceled and would not reschedule. We never met at the bank again. I repeatedly asked her for the list of the contents, which she said was being valued by a numismatist. She never sent me the inventory although she repeatedly promised to do so. As we neared the deadline to file the estate tax returns, *which ask whether the deceased had a safe deposit box*, she demanded that I prepare the tax return without reference to the safe deposit box.

I refused because I had actual knowledge that there was a safe deposit box, and I knew its contents. I would not prepare and sign an estate tax return that I knew would be fraudulent. To do so would have been felony tax fraud, and I saw no good reason to go to prison to enrich this family. Estate taxes were due so penalties and interest began to accrue. She fired me, hired a new lawyer in a large law firm, and filed a bar complaint against me. The new lawyer called me and asked for the file, and asked why I did not file the tax return. I explained the reasons, including her hand-written, signed and dated partial inventory. I sent him the entire file, with a clear conscience, knowing I had done nothing wrong. But somehow, I was wrong about being right.

The bar sent me a copy of her complaint, which I answered, including copies of all of the relevant documents. The bar decided to issue a reprimand against me for not filing the tax return. When I argued with the bar's senior prosecutor that my client was demanding that I commit fraud for her, she did not care that I chose to abide by the law by not committing fraud. She was just focused on the fact that the estate incurred penalties and interest for filing the estate tax return late. Not knowing what I know now, which is, a) that the bar *can* be beaten and, b) I should have described to her exactly where she could do with her reprimand, I was intimidated by the power of the bar and agreed to the reprimand. That was the mistake of a young lawyer still in awe of the system.

And what about the client, her new lawyer, and the fraudulent tax return? They prepared, signed, and filed it with no reference to the safe deposit box. Not knowing the difference, the state accepted it. So I was the bad guy for refusing to commit an illegal act. And the contents of the safe deposit box? Well, there was so much money that it probably took the family a long time to divide it equally, but their time was certainly well spent. Remember what I said about large firms receiving better treatment than sole practitioners? This was a textbook example.

Both bar counsel and her new lawyer knew that the tax return was fraudulent and they did nothing to prevent or correct the tax fraud and perjury. To this day, I do not understand the reason for the bar's action, except to protect one of their own: a lawyer in a large law firm. The bottom line was that the new lawyer and bar counsel both suborned the perjury and were complicit in the fraud that the executor committed when she signed the tax return.

And finally, there is the case in which the State Bar of Arizona reprimanded a lawyer even though they could not identify any specific rule or law that he violated. At the time it happened, he was a civil trial attorney representing a plaintiff in a lawsuit for damages. The defendant carried liability insurance and was represented by his insurance company's lawyers. The plaintiff's lawyer won a jury verdict of $200,000.00. When demand was made for payment the insurance company refused. He continued to demand and they continued to refuse. Finally, knowing that his paramount duty was to collect the judgment for his client, he went after the defendant's personal assets. The defendant screamed in outrage, but instead of helping to ensure that his insurance company paid the judgment against him, the defendant filed a bar complaint. Now what did the lawyer do wrong? You're right; nothing. In fact, he did everything that he should have done to vigorously represent his client, which was his primary ethical duty. He took exactly the correct action in behalf of his client. The bar could not identify or tell him what he did wrong, but that did not stop them from issuing a reprimand against him. An interesting aside: He is the same lawyer who billed in 1/100th of an hour increments.

CHAPTER SIX

Lawyers – Behind the Scenes in A Law Firm

It is necessary to understand the nature of the profession before we can explore the history or events surrounding individuals or groups of lawyers. The facts may not change your overall opinion of lawyers, but may help you see them in a different light. First, the nature of the profession: How do you get in? How do you get out? How profitable is it? How stressful? Do lawyers have different demographics than non-lawyers? And how do law firms work behind the scenes?

Chapter Seven will be devoted to a variety of different lawyers, some innocent and some not, so for each lawyer, you decide whether they were treated fairly, and whether their legal and social successes compensate for the mistakes of which they were accused.

So let's begin by understanding what it takes to become a lawyer. First, you must graduate from a fully accredited college or university with a bachelor's degree. Contrary to popular belief, the subject of the degree is rarely important. Why? Because it very rarely has any relevance to your future work as a lawyer. Then you must graduate from a fully accredited law school with either a J.D. or L.lb. degree. Different title; same degree.

At this point, you have either come from a moneyed family, incurred massive student loans, or worked your fingers to the bone by being self-supporting during the prior seven years of school. But again contrary to popular belief, fostered by the law schools themselves, law school is not an all-consuming event. At worse, it is a 40-hour per week job. In fact, while I was in law school, I always had two jobs. But there were many students who lived and breathed their classes, their homework, their research papers, etc. They worked from dawn until they fell asleep at their desk, and they did no better in school, taking the Bar Exam, and then practicing law than I and many other lawyers did.

After graduation from school, you apply to the Bar for permission to take the Bar Exam (usually two days long) and a separate ethics exam. A 'grade' does not matter – either you pass or you fail. After passing the exams, your background is investigated, and if you pass the background check by an anonymous 'character and fitness' committee, you are invited to join the bar. Congratulations are certainly in order; you have just completed a seven and one half year ordeal. But do you know what you have actually accomplished? Pure academics, plus training in a method of analysis unique to the law. But you have absolutely no idea how to practice law! You do not know how to attract clients or how to converse with them.. How, when, and how much to charge the client? How to start a case, defend a case, learn the format of pleadings, arguing motions, negotiating, addressing a judge or jury and the myriad other tasks and techniques that will give you the opportunity for success?

So how do you begin? Some brand new lawyers accept jobs with large law firms and are required to work 12 – 14 hours per day, often six days per week. A fortunate minority will eventually become partners. Others take jobs with corporations. The daily production is far less, but you are expected to maintain the appearance of long hours and hard work. Others become government employees, for which the expectations and the quality of lawyering are often quite low. And finally, many new lawyers join small firms or 'hang out their shingle'. This is the hardest path to success. Not only do they start from scratch, with no clients and no income, they have to attract new clients while learning how to represent those clients. There is no vacation, no sick days, no 401(k), no health insurance, no nothing but the hope of individual success. The failure rate is rather high.

Let's consider the sole practitioner. Every day, he must develop new clients, largely by word of mouth, do the work on the cases he has accepted, appear in court or other government proceedings, manage his office, collect his fees, and accept responsibility for everything that occurs in his office. To build his practice, he must do community work, join the chamber of commerce, enter local politics, and expand his network and his name. If there is not enough money in the till at the end of the week to pay the secretary, the phone or the rent, he makes up the difference out of his own pocket. Working all week to lose money; what a great feeling! Of course, there are those cases in which he collects a large fee, acquires a significant new client, or wins an important case. But all things considered, being a sole practitioner is the hardest way to start a law practice.

Next to consider is the small law firm of 2-20 lawyers. They differ only slightly from the sole practitioner. Their primary concern is paying the overhead and making a reasonable income for themselves. They might all be equal partners, or there might be partners and associates. They are more likely to do pro-bono work because there are other lawyers 'back at the shop' working while they are volunteering. Yet they do not normally make large contributions to bar organizations, and thus do not enjoy the same standing in the eyes of the bar as the large firms. They are more likely to be audited and complaints against them are more likely to be vigorously prosecuted.

And then there the large firms, which I consider to be any firm from twenty lawyers to as many as five hundred. Think of a great white shark feeding frenzy. Large firms are wealthy, have multiple layers of partners and of associates, paralegals, secretaries, non-lawyer administrators, couriers, etc. They are the most likely to double bill for the two lawyer meeting, or to bill for paralegals and secretaries, photocopies, postage, and the like. They are administered more as manufacturing facilities than as lawyers working and thinking independently. The politics are horrendous. Yet they are the most cherished by the bar, for their participation and contributions are enormous. Very rarely do you hear of a senior lawyer in a large firm being sanctioned by the bar for his conduct. Yet I assure you, they are as egregious in their ethical violations as any other lawyer.

CHAPTER SEVEN

(In)Famous Lawyers vs. the Legal System

I must compliment the courts and bar associations for one dubious distinction. When a famous, or infamous, lawyer is caught up in wrongdoing, or an accusation of wrongdoing, they are on the case like bees on honey. Cases that will make the news because of their notoriety (the Duke lacrosse players) and cases that will make the news because of the fame of the lawyer (F. Lee Bailey) seem to garner immediate attention and action from the bar. More routine cases, those that are neither famous nor infamous, go to the bottom of the pile. At least one state Supreme Court has already imposed a series of deadlines on its bar association so that 'justice' may be meted out more quickly. But speaking for that great unwashed majority of lawyers…..Hey, what's the hurry? We know that bar counsel earns its keep by finding us 'guilty' whenever possible.

So let's look at some of America's most famous lawyers and what got them into trouble, sometimes inadvertently, more often by their decision to take certain actions. Some results were just; others were not. These are presented in no particular order.

Clarence Darrow, the legendary and eloquent trial lawyer and spokesman for the emerging labor union movement in the early 1900's, and the man who debated William Jennings Bryant in the famous Scopes 'monkey trial', once represented two brothers accused of setting fire to a factory in a labor/management confrontation. Several people died in the fire, so the brothers were on trial for arson, murder, and their lives. After the trial, the prosecutor's office indicted Clarence Darrow on charges of suborning perjury, which he steadfastly denied. He went through a jury trial on the wrong side, as the accused, but was found 'not guilty'. Sadly, subsequent research, interviews with witnesses, and other material have proven, to a high degree of certainty, that Clarence Darrow did in fact suborn perjury by encouraging certain witnesses to testify in a manner favorable to his clients, in that case and others. Although he may have believed that he was just 'leveling the playing field', or 'representing the cause' rather than his clients, he committed numerous felonies. Even if he were alive today, he could not be tried again because that would constitute double jeopardy. But the question becomes: He fought all of his life for the poor, underprivileged working class. He was a hero and leader of the emerging labor union movement. He stands as an American icon for his skills, dedication, and remarkable success in the name of employee and union rights. Yet the reality is that he suborned perjury to win some of his cases. He was right that the playing field needed leveling, and that the prosecution was doubtless suborning perjury on its own behalf, but did the end justify his means? He was committing felonies for his perception of the public good. In a society governed by a legal system, the answer must be "*No*". Yet in a perfect world, the labor/management strife and all of its attendant conflict and violence would never have occurred, and those two brothers would have never set fire to that factory. Darrow passed away decades ago, we will never know his reasons.

Roy Cohn, one of America's most effective and most reviled lawyers, rose to fame as the lead counsel in the 1950's for Joseph McCarthy and his congressional witch-hunt for Communists. Many ethical people, staying on the high road, stood up to McCarthy and his congressional 'investigative' committee by refusing to testify or by refusing to point their finger at people who, if indeed they were members of the Communist Party, were simply exercising their Constitutional rights to the freedoms of speech and assembly. For the people who courageously defied Senator McCarthy and his lead counsel, Roy Cohn, many of their careers and lives were ruined. Roy Cohn played an integral role in this dark moment of America's history, but it gave him the national stage that he needed to become successful. After his work with Joseph McCarthy, he went on to become a successful yet controversial trial lawyer in New York City. Stories have circulated for years that if a defendant could afford his fees, all that was necessary for the defendant to beat the charges against him was to have Roy Cohn appear as his counsel. Frequently, it has been said, the judges simply dismissed the charges when Mr. Cohn appeared. It may be true or it may be part of his mystique, yet the stories persist. Again, having passed away, we will never hear of those rumors from him, and no judge who acted in that manner will ever admit it.

The New York State Bar's prosecutors were constantly nipping at his heels, looking for legal or ethical misdeeds, but were not able to make anything stick. Finally, when he was terminally ill, the New York State Bar expedited proceedings against him so that they could ensure his disbarment before his death. They succeeded. How laudable. I do not know, and cannot presume to judge, whether the ongoing harassment and eventual disbarment were justified or vindictive. I do not know or care whether Roy Cohn even cared. It is generally accepted that his arrogance, surly demeanor, and defiance led to his infamy extending far beyond Joseph McCarthy and followed him into his grave. And that defiance was the reason he was both respected and reviled.

F. Lee Bailey is a contemporary example of how far one can fall, rightly or wrongly, at the hands of a legal system that discourages effective defense representation and punishes lawyers who are successful. Mr. Bailey's very presence and speech were electrifying. His skills as a trial lawyer are the stuff of which legends are made. His ability to conduct cross-examinations was legendary, and has rarely been or ever will be matched. His eloquence in closing arguments was equally brilliant. He gained fame for representing Albert DiSalvo, the man widely believed to be the Boston Strangler. He gained fame for championing the use of polygraph tests (lie detectors) and their use in Court. He represented Patricia Hearst when she was accused of colluding with the Symbionese Liberation Army during a bank robbery and murder of a police officer. He represented Dr. Sam Shepard, and gained him a new trial in which he was acquitted. That case was the inspiration for the television series and the movie "The Fugitive". Later in his career, he was brought in as part of O. J. Simpson's defense team for the sole purpose of conducting cross-examinations. He stands as a contemporary icon among the American legal community. But too much praise, or time spent in the public eye, or publicity can add pressure and expectations that do not haunt most other lawyers.

Mr. Bailey's downfall came while protecting his client's constitutional right to be represented by counsel of his own choosing, and counsel's right to be fairly compensated for his work. The adversary, of course, was the U. S. government. Here's what happened.

The U.S. Government, and many of the states, have laws that allow for the assets of a defendant to be seized and forfeited to the government. This is particularly true in drug smuggling, distribution and possession cases. This is not done in an effort to reduce any governmental deficit or to reduce the national debt. The effect on the governmental deficit or spending is miniscule. It is done to impose additional penalties on defendants accused, but not yet convicted, of certain crimes. It is often done before trial, while they are still presumed innocent. It is intended to punish them twice, both by imprisonment and fines, as well as by impoverishing them. But prosecutors have taken the concept too far. By arguing that the fees paid by a defendant to his lawyer also constitute assets that are subject to forfeiture, because they presumably came from the defendant's 'illegal' activities, many prosecutors request the courts to order defense lawyers to turn their legal fees over to the government.

In Florida, Mr. Bailey was hired to represent a man accused of multiple drug offenses. His client paid him with bearer bonds that Mr. Bailey held in a Swiss bank. The prosecutors asked for an order that the bonds be forfeited to the government, before trial, which would either force Mr. Bailey to work for free (which he had no obligation to do) or to cause his client to accept the representation of a public defender or a less skilled lawyer. In any event, the clear intent was to deny his client representation by Mr. Bailey. The judge ordered Mr. Bailey to forfeit the bonds to the government. Mr. Bailey refused, and rightly so. The judge found him in contempt of court for refusing to comply with the order. The battle became more intense and more personal. After all, it was a prosecutor's dream to defeat the legendary F. Lee Bailey, and further, it became a battle of wills between the judge and Mr. Bailey. Of course, the issue was appealed and Mr. Bailey eventually lost. The Florida State Bar filed ethical charges against him, and eventually those charges led to his disbarment. His was an enormous fall from a legendary career into ignominy. Now think what you will of drug crimes, particularly on a large scale, and think what you will of those criminal defense lawyers who represent defendants charged with substantial drug crimes. But the clear fact remains that F. Lee Bailey was disbarred for defending and protecting his client's constitutional right to counsel and for insisting that he had a right to be paid for representing that client. He is neither the first nor the only lawyer to be punished by the government for protecting their clients' constitutional rights.

It is an embarrassment to America, but as a sitting president, Bill Clinton was found to have lied to a grand jury about his affairs (grand juries decide, by hearing only the prosecution's side of a case, whether to charge, or indict, a person with a crime). He was impeached by the House of Representatives and tried by the U. S. Senate. He was acquitted and remained in the White House until the end of his term. But the Arkansas State Bar saw the matter differently, and he has the distinction to be the only president to have his law license suspended for five (5) years while he was the sitting president.

Hillary Clinton, also a member of the Arkansas Bar, narrowly escaped similar treatment by testifying repeatedly that ***"She did not know"***, or that ***"She could not remember"***, and so on, in regard to the numerous scandals and mysteries in which the Bill Clinton administration was embroiled. But there are still several mysteries that Hillary Clinton can explain yet refuses to do so. For example, how did she make a profit in one day on the Chicago Commodities Exchange that was larger than mathematically possible? The one that I find most galling, because it is so clearly not true, is the dispute over her Rose law firm billing records. She was subpoenaed to produce the records before an investigative grand jury or congressional committee and adamantly insisted that, despite an exhaustive search, the records could not be located. Yet within days of the expiration of the subpoena, those very same records miraculously appeared on a table *in the residential section of the White House.* A miracle! But she will not explain that miracle except to opine that a member of the domestic staff found the records and set them on the table for her. And as you know, she was a serious contender for the 2008 Democratic nomination for President, has served four years as the U. S. Secretary of State, and is the presumptive democratic nominee for president in 2016.

Some lawyers have their fall from grace by deliberate and intentional crimes committed for their own benefit. The Richard Nixon and Spiro Agnew debacles represent the ultimate examples of corruption and illegality in high places. While serving as governor of Maryland, before becoming Vice-President, Spiro Agnew was accepting bribes to do favors for his friends and benefactors. He lied about it under oath. He was indicted, convicted, and sentenced to prison. He was disbarred. He resigned from the vice-residency in disgrace solely as a result of his own greed. There is nothing new about lawyers committing crimes solely for greed, but Americans have a right to expect that it not happen with a man who sits one chair away from the presidency. Speaking of which, Richard Nixon's own crimes are well documented, and he became the first president to resign in the middle of his term to avoid impeachment. He spent the rest of his life in disgrace, but regained some of his credibility as time went by and Americans began to understand his excellent diplomatic skills and the good that he had done for the country in the arena of foreign affairs. But his career was permanently ended by his greed. Not for money, but for power.

It is only fair to remind everyone that the next president, Gerald Ford, also an attorney, sacrificed his political career by granting a pardon to Richard Nixon. Although wildly unpopular at the time, President Ford had the foresight and the wisdom to know that America needed to move beyond Watergate rather than spend several more years mired in its filth. It was preventing Americans from leaving history behind them. And that could only be accomplished with a pardon that would remove Nixon and Watergate from the news forever. So Mr. Ford had a very short presidency that may not have comported with the country's emotional expectations, but was exactly what America needed to begin healing. History has borne out his wisdom. He is remembered as an honest and courageous man, perhaps the most courageous president since Abraham Lincoln.

Oftentimes, unknown lawyers find themselves disgraced or disbarred as a result of their own actions. It is only the public revelation of their wrongdoing that makes them household names, or at least gives them their *"15 minutes of fame"*. An excellent example is the North Carolina county prosecutor, Mike NiFong, who sought to prosecute several Duke lacrosse players for rape. An elected official, he was facing a strong challenge in the next election and desperately needed to win the Duke case. That may or may not be the reason for his actions in this well-known case, but we do know that his attempted prosecution of the three lacrosse players led him from anonymity to a presence on the national stage to disbarment and disgrace. The facts are: At a fraternity party, the students hired a stripper to perform for them; not an uncommon activity at fraternity parties. Afterward, she accused three of the students of raping her, claiming she was not hired as a prostitute but only as a stripper. There was an immediate public outrage, and the righteous Mike NiFong, as the county attorney, personally led the investigation and prosecution. He was widely hailed for his vigorous efforts to seek justice for this poor, victimized woman.

But then problems began to develop within his case. He made several very inappropriate and prejudicial remarks to the media regarding the young mens' guilt and the credibility of the victim. Appropriate prosecutorial conduct (remember the 'right to a fair trial' concept?) would have been to make no public statements, but he did otherwise. Secondly, the 'victim's statements began to vary and by the time the case was finally dismissed by the North Carolina's attorney general, she had made several inconsistent statements. But the straw that broke Mike NiFong's back was the issue of the DNA evidence. DNA samples, including semen, were taken from the woman's body and from the three lacrosse players that Mike NiFong indicted. The results came back and Mr. NiFong did not make full disclosure of the results to either the defense lawyers or to the court. There is an absolute rule, in all American courts, that in a criminal case the prosecution must turn over all exculpatory ('tending to show innocence') evidence to the defense counsel. Mike NiFong did not tell the defense counsel that the DNA test results found no DNA from any of the young men on or in the woman's body, and further, that another man's semen was found in the woman's body but it's DNA codes did not match any of the defendants.

Furthermore, he lied to the Court in the investigation of the issue, and a representative from the DNA testing laboratory testified that Mr. NiFong instructed the laboratory to only report certain results rather than all of the results. When this information came to light, the North Carolina attorney general's office took control of the case. Mr. NiFong resigned, was charged with serious ethical violations by the State Bar, and was very quickly tried and immediately disbarred.

In Arizona, which is often referred to as 'Arizona Territory' for its frontier-style justice and lack of laws in many areas (after all, it did not become a state until 1912), we have several examples of otherwise unknown lawyers and judges who have self-destructed. Our male Governors seem to resign in disgrace or to be indicted, while our female Governors do not. In fact, those women are held in high regard. Now don't get me wrong. Female lawyers are capable of being as dishonest and unethical as male lawyers, but for some reason the ethics of Arizona governors seem to be defined by gender only. Maybe women should rule the world. Or at least Arizona.

One of Arizona's preeminent personal injury lawyers found himself in a position that every attorney dreads: punishment for his own stupidity. He accepted a case in behalf of numerous tenants in an apartment complex who claimed that the untreated mold in their apartments was causing illness and harming them. As in all personal injury cases, Harold Hyams asked for mega dollars in his lawsuit, and then his problems began.

The case was not as good as he had first believed, but he soldiered on, trying to create a settlement or a jury verdict that would benefit his clients. But Mr. Hyams filed frivolous motions that were denied, missed court appearances that he had scheduled, filed motions for rehearing when his original frivolous motions had been denied, and engaged in multiple instances of other inappropriate behavior. His behavior as a lawyer was unprofessional and surprising to everyone who knew him. This went on for a substantial period of time as all parties watched the case deteriorate, but apparently that just caused Mr. Hyams to dig in his heels. He continued to cause so many delays, waste so much time, and pursue matters that had already been decided, that ultimately the lawyers for the defendants petitioned the court for reimbursement of their legal fees because Mr. Hyams' tactics were so egregiously inappropriate. After a hearing, he was ordered to personally reimburse the defense lawyers $750,000.00 in legal fees, and the judge herself filed an ethical complaint with the State Bar asking for an investigation. The State Bar censured him and placed him on two years of probation, with strict limitations regarding his future use of the appellate courts.

Mr. Hyams has a very successful and lucrative law practice, but risked throwing it all away because of his unprofessional behavior in just one case.

The Pima County attorney's office (the county prosecutors) was so rife with documented corruption that it became a public embarrassment. The problem is exacerbated by the elected county attorney, Barbara LaWall, who often publicly defends the actions and innocence of her employees even when their illegal or ethical problems are proven. She would be well advised to open her eyes and act expeditiously and fairly when a problem becomes apparent. But then again, she is just a politician.

The first problem to enter the public awareness involved her senior criminal prosecutor and a Tucson police officer. Ken Peasley, the prosecutor, was prosecuting a young man for first-degree murder, and was seeking the death penalty. During the course of the trial, he asked the police officer a question to which the defense objected. The defendant was convicted and sentenced to death. The Supreme Court ordered a retrial and the exclusion of that question. A second trial was held, and Mr. Peasley asked *exactly* the same question and the police officer gave *exactly* the same answer. Again, the defendant was convicted and sentenced to death. At this point, disciplinary proceedings were instituted against Mr. Peasley and he was disbarred. His audacity to defy a Supreme Court decision *in a death penalty case* was appalling. Mr. Peasley has since passed away and another outstanding career was thrown away.

David White, another senior and successful prosecutor in Barbara LaWall's office, died tragically at a young age. He was well-respected.

But after his sudden death, as his cases were being reassigned, the other prosecutors found numerous examples in which he withheld exculpatory evidence from defense counsel as well as other unethical or illegal acts. That affected many pending cases, and caused a review of many cases that he handled in the past, many of which were dismissed.

The Pima County Attorney's office faced even more problems. Lourdes Lopez, a prosecutor in the office, quit when she learned that she and her boyfriend were to be named in a federal indictment alleging that her boyfriend, Dr. Bradley Schwartz, was writing prescriptions to Lopez and others to obtain drugs for himself. But the worst was yet to come. Later, Schwartz was indicted for the murder of his former partner, Dr. David Stidham. Schwartz hired a hit man to kill Stidman and make it look like a parking lot mugging. The evidence was compelling that Lopez knew of the plan prior to the murder and did nothing to prevent it. Further, it was determined that she told three confidants in the County Attorneys' office what she knew and none of them warned law-enforcement officials. Lopez and Schwartz eventually settled their drug indictment by agreeing to probation and community service. But Schwartz and the hit man were convicted of murder and are serving life sentences. Lopez was disbarred, but in a conversation with her, she told me she has every intention of regaining her license and resuming her practice of law. I doubt she will find it easy.

Milberg Weiss, a San Diego based law firm specializing in class action cases was found to have repeatedly solicited false plaintiffs so that a lawsuit could be filed. Those 'clients' were compensated for their willingness to be a named plaintiff. In fact, some of those laymen and women became professional plaintiffs that were named in several lawsuits as lead plaintiffs. In other words, the firm was fraudulently creating its own lawsuits and clients. The result was prison terms for some of the senior partners.

Let there be no doubt – there are countless other examples of (In) famous lawyers and politicians, well known, whose misdeeds have led to their downfall. These are just some examples.

CHAPTER EIGHT

Why Do Attorneys Have Such A Bad Reputation?

Because they earned it. Lawyering, particularly in the private sector, is not an easy business. Lawyers have an unusually high rate of addiction and divorce, and a lower life expectancy than the general population. The public's opinion of lawyers is so low that I experienced a case where my attorney was actually afraid to call other lawyers as expert witnesses in my behalf.

Here's what happened. I was hired by two brothers who owned a piece of land and planned to build a house for themselves. They needed a construction loan for the house, and they wanted it done yesterday, which meant a title search had to be done. Again. So I went to the office of land records and began the title search. It was virtually impossible. No modern survey had ever been done and the land was compromised of several parcels. Many parts of rural New England have land that has been in the same family for generations, and their ownership often began with a land grant from the King of England – usually for service in the French and Indian War. The parcel descriptions in the old deeds included such wording as "200 paces from the north side of the road to the oak tree that is 6 inches in diameter; thence 300 paces to the large rock whose sharpest slope points to the north, and thence.....". You get the idea. So I went to the well-respected real estate lawyer who did the title search when the brothers bought the land, and who had certified the title as good and clear, and he gave me consent to rely upon his work.

My clients' construction loan was closed. After the house was partially built, we were informed that a local political activist had purchased one of the parcels that my clients believed they had purchased. A furious round of negotiations ensued, and a land swap was negotiated which appeared to satisfy all parties. But it was not to be.

While helping my clients negotiate a solution, I advised them not to notify the title insurance company of the problem because the bank would immediately freeze the construction loan and they would be unable to finish the house. They agreed. After the settlement was reached, the brothers found a lawyer willing to sue me for negligence. I contacted my malpractice insurance company and they assigned my defense to a skilled defense lawyer. He found four well-respected real estate lawyers willing to testify in my defense – that I had handled the entire matter correctly. After the trial began, the insurance company got cold feet and wanted to settle. The settlement was for $80,000. And why did they get cold feet when our defense was so solid and supported by the experts in real estate law? For the simple reason that they feared the jury might view the experts as a conspiracy of lawyers supporting another lawyer – me – and award the brothers an unreasonably high amount of money even though I was right. In other words, the insurance company, that insured a lawyer, was scared to use lawyers as expert witnesses. The final result? The brothers got their house and an extra $80,000. Their lawyer simply saw an opportunity to take a case that was essentially extortion, and he probably received one-third of the $80,000.

There exists a hypocrisy and dishonesty among lawyers that they have created for themselves. They present themselves as noble, honest and dedicated to justice and serving their clients vigorously, yet they frequently do the opposite. They used to be called the 'noble profession' with the blindfolded lady and her lopsided scales of justice; yet they are viewed in exactly the opposite way. They are uncivil to one another, ethical rules are commonly violated, and they allow their clients to commit perjury. I do not mean to suggest that all lawyers behave in this way; in fact, many do not. Yet these practices are becoming more common. The real goal is to win, make as much money as possible, and enhance their reputations. So without getting caught they will often do whatever is necessary to achieve their goals. All else is secondary.

Many people (often Republicans; trial lawyers are major contributors to the Democratic Party, which resists caps on damage awards) condemn the occasional verdicts of several million dollars and the award of billions of dollars in punitive (read: punishment) damages. They blame the plaintiffs' lawyers and runaway juries. But this does not happen nearly as often as the insurance companies would have you believe, and in fact they and their insured clients are often responsible for the expense of litigation and the size of those verdicts. Consider: When an insurance company receives notice that one of their insureds is being sued, they refer the defense of the case to an outside law firm. The firm chosen to represent the insurance company has two motives in handling the case. The first is to bill as many hours as possible, knowing that their bills will be paid by the company. We have previously discussed legal bills, with double billing, travel billing, associate and paralegal billing, and copies, postage and fax costs. Their second motive is to do as much as possible so that they have no liability if and when they lose the case. Litigation is a modern, yet barely civilized, form of warfare.

Government lawyers are no different. They have well-paying jobs, retirement plans, health insurance, wield tremendous power over others, and are rarely accountable to the public. A lawyer friend, about whom I have previously talked, once worked in-house for the Social Security

Administration dealing with disability claims. He put in no more than the normal office hours, including lunch and breaks. After a few months, he was called into his supervisor's office and bluntly told to slow down. When he said that he was simply working at his normal pace and expected hours per day, he was told that he was processing four (4!) times as much as work as the other lawyers in the office. The supervisor had set an expectation that each lawyer complete only two cases per month, and he was accomplishing four times that. He was making the rest of the other lawyers look bad. So rather than demand that the other lawyers be more productive, he was told to slow down to meet the 'expectations' of his job. He left shortly thereafter. And who paid these lazy government lawyers? You, me and the taxpayers who were trying to have their disability claims approved.

Our litigious society has enabled lawyers to create two more specialties: lawyers who sue lawyers and lawyers who defend lawyers, on issues such as negligence, breach of contract, and ethical violations. Lawyers are creating more litigation, which leads to the need for more lawyers, more courthouses, more public support staff, etc. Lawyers, together with legislatures, have created a monster that shows no signs of diminishing.

Another example: Several years ago, an attorney friend negotiated a plea agreement for his client, which involved several misdemeanors. The assistant prosecutor handling the case made the verbal agreement with him, so the judge set a date on which he would accept the plea agreement and impose the sentence.

When that date arrived, the prosecutor arrived in court with her witnesses in tow and told my friend that she was ready for trial. Stunned, he reminded her of their plea agreement, and furthermore, that he did not bring witnesses to court or prepare for trial because they had an agreement. She claimed that she told him she had no authority to make that agreement and that it had just been a proposal. She claimed that her supervisor had vetoed the agreement. When he objected vehemently to the court, and she responded with equal vehemence that she was justified, the judge rescheduled the hearing and advised both lawyers that they were going to testify regarding their discussions and whether she had misrepresented her authority. Only then would the judge decide whether to accept the plea agreement or reschedule the case for trial.

Because he was the attorney for the defendant, ethics and common sense both dictated that my friend should not be the person to cross-examine the prosecutor. He asked me to cross-examine her, which I happily agreed to do. This was a wonderful and rare opportunity: the chance to cross-examine a prosecutor under oath. There were five issues for the court to decide. First, did she have authority to make the agreement? Second, if she had the authority, did she actually make the agreement? If the court found the answer to these questions to be "Yes", then the agreement would be binding and accepted by the court. The third issue was whether she had the authority, had made the agreement, and was now reneging, which would have resulted in the court accepting the agreement. And fourth, did she make the agreement but misrepresent her authority to do so, which if found to be true, would present her with a serious ethical problem (fraud upon the court, which can result in suspension or disbarment), and would cause the agreement to be accepted. And finally, did she have authority but decide to renege without telling the defense lawyer in an effort at one-upmanship? Again, if that was the case, the agreement would be accepted. In other words, did she attempt to deceive him that the agreement was still good when she intended to go to trial? The only way that the court would reject the agreement was to find that no agreement had been made, or she had clearly stated that she needed supervisory approval. The burden of proof was on her.

When the day came, I called her to the witness stand and asked the court to declare her to be a hostile witness (because I called her as my witness, I needed the court's consent to cross-examine her as a hostile witness, which is commonly granted). She took the witness stand with an angry and hostile attitude as if to say, *"Who was I to question a prosecutor's integrity?"* The answer was that we had every right to do so. She did not deny making the agreement but insisted that she told my friend that needed approval.

My cross-examination was aggressive, but her arrogance and anger were obvious, and she had no proof that she ever told him the agreement was provisional or was rejected. Her attitude belied her words and her integrity was severely damaged. When my friend called himself to the witness stand, he calmly explained to the judge precisely what their conversations had been, and that she never acknowledged a lack of authority or contacted him to advise that the agreement was off.

Based on the testimony, and the demeanor of the two attorneys that testified, the court ruled immediately: The plea agreement was binding because she had represented that she had full authority to make the agreement. Her subsequent lies did her no good.

CHAPTER NINE

The Bill Of Rights

In 1787, the Constitutional Congress wrote, and in 1788, New Hampshire became the ninth state (of 12) to ratify the United States Constitution. It is breath-taking in both its brevity and its scope. In just a few pages, it created a federal government for the new United States of America. It is without doubt the greatest legal document ever written, and created the structure for the finest government ever created. Not since the Magna Carta was first signed in 1215 by King John of England, and later reaffirmed by King Edward I in 1297, has any empowering document taken such far-reaching steps towards democracy.

The U. S. Constitution was so well conceived that it has been amended only twenty seven times, and two of those imposed and revoked Prohibition. There have only been twenty five substantive amendments.

But when our forefathers wrote the Constitution, they neglected to include within it the very reason that the Revolutionary War was fought – to preserve those freedoms which had been granted to Englishmen five centuries before in the Magna Carta and to grant other freedoms as set forth in the Bill of Rights. Its genesis was the Magna Carta.

The Magna Carta was the first time that the King of England made himself and 'his heirs forever' subject to the law, and granted to all 'freemen' of England the rights and liberties of the kingdom. It provides, in pertinent part, that:

> *"No freemen shall be taken, imprisoned....or in any other way destroyed....except by the lawful judgment of his peers, or by the law of the land. To no one will we sell, to none will we deny or delay right or justice."*

When Englishmen began migrating to the new world, and established the original colonies, they brought with them the Magna Carta and declared that it granted them in America the same rights they possessed in England. It was only after several generations, when the English throne had consistently denied those rights, and sent its army to quell disruptions, that the Declaration of Independence was written and signed, and the Revolutionary War broke out. The colonists were fighting first for those rights and liberties which had been granted to them almost five centuries before, but also of necessity, for independence from an unjust England and to create a new nation in the 'new world'.

In 1791, the first ten amendments to the Constitution were enacted by Congress and ratified by three-quarters of the states. Those ten amendments have come to be called the Bill of Rights because they guaranteed those individual liberties and freedoms, and much more.

But the Constitution was still imperfect. The Bill of Rights applied only to the federal government. It did not apply to the states, territories, counties and municipalities of America. Not until 1867, when the nation approved the 14th amendment, did it apply to all forms of government, and more notably, protect our freedoms and rights from all levels of government.

Now let me be clear about the ongoing existence of our Bill of Rights. The only group in the country that has successfully fought for and protected it is the criminal defense lawyers. Not the American Civil Liberties Union, which concerns itself more with civil rights than civil liberties. Not the courts of their own volition. Certainly not law enforcement personnel. And not any city council, county government, state legislature, congress, or president. Look no further than the Patriot Act to understand what I mean. I say this because government and law enforcement, at all levels, sees these rights and freedoms as an interference to the exercise of their powers and authority. Those pesky rights! They interfere with the smooth and easy control of the populace, which is the purpose of law. But without them, we may as well revert to an England before the Magna Carta or to the Star Chambers of the Spanish Inquisition.

No one else in the world enjoys the rights that we are granted, but understand that governments at all levels seek to ignore them and take them away. It is the criminal defense lawyers who have preserved them.

So let's look at each of the ten amendments to see what protection and freedoms they give us.

First Amendment

"Congress shall make no law respecting an establishment of religion, or prohibiting the free exercise thereof; or abridging the freedom of speech, or of the press; or the right of the people peaceably to assemble, and to petition the Government for a redress of grievances."

The U. S. Supreme Court has ruled that the rights to freedom of speech, press and religion were coupled in a single guaranty with the right of the people peaceably to assemble and to petition for redress of grievances not by accident or coincidence, but that all these, though not identical, are inseparable and are cognate rights. Thomas v. Collins (1945) 65 S. Ct. 315,

323 U.S. 516. Any attempt to restrict free speech or free assembly must be justified by clear public interest threatened not doubtfully, but by clear and present danger, and the rational connection between the remedy provided and the evil to be curbed, which in other contexts might support legislation against attack on due process grounds, will not suffice. See <u>Thomas</u>, above.

Thus, the five essential rights of the 1st Amendment, although separate and distinct, are all to be treated and enforced equally.

But that is not always done. For example, bar associations have violated the 1st Amendment rights of lawyers on numerous occasions, and were then reversed by the U.S. Supreme Court. Arizona did it with the issue of lawyer advertising and again with the refusal of an applicant to the Bar to disclose her political affiliation (she was a member of the Communist party). Illinois did it with the freedom of assembly, and California, Kentucky and Ohio have all found themselves with the same problem – Supreme Court reversal of their violations of lawyers' 1st Amendment rights.

The Lake Superior State University publishes an annual *'List of Words Banished from the Queen's English for Mis-Use, Over-Use, and General Uselessness'*. What? Words are banished from the language because a college committee does not like them? But the annual list is obviously tongue-in-cheek. Except for one unidentified Arizona Supreme Court judge who is said to have sent a letter to the university spokesman stating that he posted that year's list on a bulletin board and was prohibiting all attorneys from using those words. Is he kidding? Doesn't a state supreme court judge understand the rudimentary concept of the right of free speech?

A few years ago, Larry Flynt, the publisher of Hustler magazine, appeared on the Piers Morgan talk show. Mr. Flynt's greatest accomplishment was not building a graphic pornographic empire, but rather taking his criminal conviction for selling pornography to the Supreme Court, which reversed his felony conviction on the grounds that Hustler magazine, while offensive to most people, is nevertheless an exercise of free speech, and therefore it is not a crime to publicize and distribute the magazine. It remains a landmark ruling.

Piers Morgan asked Mr. Flynt if he still believed that shouting "FIRE" in a crowded building ought not be considered free speech. Mr. Flynt responded that he had changed his view on that, stating that anything said should be protected under the 1st Amendment, but that the person who abuses the right of free speech should be held accountable for his actions. His rationale? If you begin to find exceptions to such a powerful right, then you have begun the process of eroding that right, and once the erosion begins, it does not stop. I was surprised to hear that answer, but upon reflection, I have to agree with him. Larry Flynt may be despicable to most people, but he is definitely a man who lives and fights for his principles. His valuable contribution to America was the protection of offensive free speech.

As to the other 1st Amendment rights, the federal government is forbidden from establishing an official national religion, and every individual is entitled to practice the religion of their choice. Freedom of the press is guaranteed, although often abused. The right to peacefully assemble necessarily includes the right to choose not to assemble with a particular group, but time and time again, we have seen law-enforcement violently, and sometimes lethally, seek to break up free assemblies. Just in our life time, the Ohio National Guard fired live ammunition at the Kent State protesters, killing four. Mayor Daley, during the 1968 Democratic National Convention in Chicago, used deadly force to quell assemblies by anti-Vietnam War protesters. We are watched as various cities across the county used force to break up peaceful assemblies of the 'Occupy' movement. Now, peaceful demonstrations are often broken up by militarized police. It has often been said that any person has the right to say anything, no matter how repugnant to the listener and that our 1st Amendment rights are worth dying to protect.

This very short discussion of the 1st Amendment cannot begin to do justice to everything contained in this succinct sentence that is this amendment. It would take volumes to discuss everything found in the 1st. Suffice it to say that it is the bedrock on which our other rights rest and it is our first defense against tyranny.

Second Amendment

"A well-regulated militia, being necessary to the security of a free State, the right of the people to keep and bear arms, shall not be infringed."

Any one reading this is aware of the constant and emotional issue of gun control that rages across the nation. So let's dissect the meaning of the 2nd Amendment. First, what is the dictionary definition of 'militia'? According to Webster's unabridged Dictionary (2nd Ed.), it is *"A body of citizen soldiers as distinguished from professional soldiers"* or *"A body of citizens organized in a paramilitary group and typically regarding themselves as defenders of individual rights against the presumed interference of the federal government"*.

So why was it important to include the right of the citizenry to have a well-regulated militia? Because that is exactly how the Revolutionary War was won. The Continental Army developed under the command of George Washington, but in every colony there were militias of citizens who banded together and fought against the British army and its German mercenaries. And how were they able to do so? Because they had they kept and used their own firearms. At that time, no one even questioned the right of a person to own firearms for protection, hunting or both. The necessity of gun ownership in private hands, as opposed to the control and possession of firearms by only the government, was a lesson well learned during the Revolutionary War.

Recently, an argument of gun control advocates is that the 2nd Amendment refers only to the weapons of that time: flintlock rifles and pistols, swords, knives and tomahawks. But those were the only weapons that the British army had as well. As firearms have evolved in sophistication, the government has accumulated them by the millions. Are we able to raise a militia and fight against our current government using the weapons of the 1700's? Of course not. Therefore it is more reasonable to interpret the 2nd Amendment as allowing us to own whatever weapons the government owns. No other reasoning allows the 2nd Amendment to remain viable.

I believe that all gun control laws are inherently unconstitutional. As for the recent problem with automatic weapons and machine guns being used by the drug and human smuggling cartels, many of which can be traced to the United States, and many of which were allowed to be transported across the U.S. - Mexico border with the full knowledge and approval of the Department of Justice, again the answer is not to restrict the right of Americans to own those weapons. The answer is to secure the border to prevent the flow of guns south, which will help in the battle against smuggling drugs and people north.

Don't tread on me!

Third Amendment

"No soldier shall, in time of peace, be quartered in any house, without the consent of the owner, nor in time of war, but in a manner to be prescribed by law."

I believe that the 3rd Amendment is self-explanatory, but it gives me an occasion to tell an interesting and little known part of American history.

As the Revolutionary War ended, America fell into a severe depression. European and upper class American war lenders were demanding repayment, and refused to take 'specie', being the new American paper money. They demanded payment in silver or gold. The courts consistently sided with the creditors and many poor families, many of them veterans, had their houses and possessions seized, and were often imprisoned for failure to pay their debts.

One such unfortunate person was Daniel Shays, a poor farmer from western Massachusetts. He fought at the battles of Lexington, Bunker Hill and Saratoga. In 1780, wounded, he returned home and immediately found himself in court for unpaid debts. He took great umbrage and began advocating for debt relief for himself and his fellow soldiers.

Word of his campaign spread and he soon had several hundred followers, most of them poor farmers and all of them armed. They formed a militia, and often seized courthouses to prevent judges from taking the bench to enforce the collection laws. Protests spread, and Massachusetts declared the 'rebels' to be treasonous.

A farmer named Plough Jagger expressed it perfectly:

> *"I have been greatly abused, have been obliged to do more than my part in the war, been loaded with class rates, town rates, province rates, Continental rates and all rates...been pulled and hauled by sheriffs, constables and collectors, and had my cattle sold for less than they were worth... The great men are going to get all we have and I think it is time for us to rise and put a stop to it, and have no more courts, nor collectors, nor lawyers."*

Wow! And whoever said that if you fail to learn from history, you are doomed to repeat it? Does this sound at all like today's America where we appear to be devolving into only two classes?

The Daniel Shays rebellion became sporadically violent, but reached its apex when Shays decided to storm the Springfield, MA armory on

January 25, 1787, and seize all of the munitions. Despite the adamant orders of Secretary of War Henry Knox to the contrary, the soldiers in the army fired their cannons at Shays' militia, killing a few. The militia fled north along the Connecticut River and encamped in Amherst. The next night, Daniel Shays forced his militia to march twenty miles through a blizzard to Petersham, MA. The fledgling U.S Army had taken up residence in the houses along West Street (the 3rd Amendment did not yet exist). At dawn on February 4, 1787, Daniel Shays and his men began the fight along West Street, routing the soldiers from the houses, with both sides progressing towards the town common. There, the general skirmish was fought. Daniel Shays lost and the government won. One month later all hostilities ceased and the rebellion ended.

Many of Daniel Shays' 'rebels' were fined, imprisoned and sentenced to death. Two were hanged. In 1788, the Governor of Massachusetts declared a general amnesty. Daniel Shays died in 1825, poor and obscure. But no doubt a very proud man. And rightly so.

On February 4, 1987, the 200th anniversary of the Petersham battle was fully reenacted. By a delightful quirk of fate, I lived on West Street in Petersham and watched the entire reenactment, with militia and soldiers fighting their way up the street, ending with the fight on the town Common. What a wonderful view into history and the American tradition of standing up against the tyranny of both the government and the law.

Fourth Amendment

"The right of the people to be secure in their person, houses, papers, and effects, against unreasonable searches and seizures, shall not be violated, and no warrants shall issue, but upon probable cause, supported by oath and affirmation, and particularly

describing the place to be searched, and the persons or things to be seized."

It is an understatement to say that this is one of the most litigated amendments, and one of the most fundamental in protecting Americans from the intrusive self-righteousness of all law enforcement agencies. That is why there is so much litigation, and appellate reviews, of rulings made under this amendment.

This is the amendment that guarantees our right to be exempt from unreasonable and intrusive searches by law-enforcement by requiring that searches be conducted only after a judge issues a search warrant, which must be supported by a law-enforcement affidavit, and must particularly describe the place to be searched, and the person or things to be seized. The exception is when police have 'probable cause' and there is not time to obtain a search warrant. Those situations arise when police are in pursuit of a person or there is a real risk that evidence will be destroyed or concealed.

You can only imagine the extent to which this requirement is abused by law-enforcement. False affidavits are routine. Exculpatory information is not included. The searches exceed the places to be searched, and the police take property and make arrests based on evidence of other crimes which the search warrant has not authorized. Police claim to see things in plain view that were not. But of course, there are exceptions. The amendment only refers to our house, our person, and our effects. So vehicles are subjected to more extensive, and legal, searches than are houses. Offices, including law offices, are not accorded the same privacy rights as are houses, including information protected by the attorney- client privilege. And any act done in public has no right of privacy whatsoever.

One sheriff's deputy told me that he would arrest me if I took the Fifth Amendment. I defied him to arrest me. So he did when I refused to allow him to enter my house. To the credit of the rookie that he was 'training', and who remembered from the police academy that we do have a Constitution, the sergeant relented and released me after one hour in handcuffs. To this day, the deputies of that department and I look askance at one another. I do not trust them to avoid fabrication, and they know that I will relentlessly pursue them if they attempt to harass my family or me. Many times I have stopped to watch as two or three squad cars surround one motorist, just to see if they are respecting his rights. Several times the officers have ordered me to leave, which I refuse to do. I am on public property and their public conduct is subject to scrutiny. In fact, it is a citizen's duty to observe police officers at work to ensure that they act properly towards our fellow Americans. They usually relent and leave me alone. Bad police officers want their actions to be shielded from public scrutiny. Good police officers have nothing to hide. Our system cannot survive in secrecy.

Fifth Amendment

"No person shall be held to answer for a capital, or otherwise infamous crime, unless on a presentment or indictment of a Grand Jury, except in cases arising in the land or naval forces, or in the militia, when in actual service in time of war or public danger; nor shall any person be subject for the same offense to be twice put in jeopardy of life or limb; nor shall be compelled in any criminal case to be a witness against himself, nor be deprived of life, liberty, or property, without due process of law; nor shall private property be taken for public use without just compensation."

The Fifth Amendment guarantees several important rights, perhaps the most famous being the right to remain silent. The U. S. Supreme Court has ruled that a person does not have to answer questions by law-enforcement officers and must be read their Miranda rights. These are:

"You have the right to remain silent. Anything you say can and will be used against you in a court of law. You have the right to an attorney. If you cannot afford an attorney, one will be provided for you."

Then police officers are required to ask the following questions:

"Do you understand each of these rights I have explained to you?"
"Having these rights in mind do you wish to speak to me?"

Some states require additional wording or advisements, but what I have quoted above is the minimum requirement when a police officer makes an arrest or holds someone 'in custody', meaning they are not free to leave. Some explanations are necessary. First, the person being held has the absolute right to a) waive their rights and speak with the officer or b) to remain silent. If they choose to speak, they can stop at any time and "take the 5th". They have a right to be represented by counsel at all times. If they speak to officers, and then decide that they want an attorney present, the interrogation must stop until an attorney is present. The arrestee has the right to confer with counsel prior to any further questioning, and has the right to have the attorney present during any further questioning. Further, the attorney has the right to instruct his client not to answer specific questions or to discuss a specific subject. In practice, the attorney almost always advises the client to not say anything at all to law-enforcement. Since most people being interrogated by a police officer don't know when to shut up, it's sound advice.

The 5th Amendment also provides for other very important rights. The first is the prohibition against double jeopardy, meaning that you cannot be tried for the same crime twice. If the prosecution loses and you are acquitted, the state has no right of appeal. Even if further evidence comes to light that proves your guilt, you cannot be retried.

The next right is that of due process. All people, in all court proceedings, whether criminal or civil, have the right to receive notice and an opportunity to be heard. Thus, if there is a matter before the court which involves your rights, you are entitled to be notified of the hearing and an opportunity to be heard at that hearing.

The final right conferred by the 5th Amendment is the right of eminent domain, (actually the right to resist eminent domain) meaning that the government cannot take your property, whether real estate or other property, without compensating you for the fair value of the property, which can be either decided by agreement, or decided by a court. In recent years, civil forfeitures have led police to seize property, usually cash, without probable cause, an arrest, or a conviction. Several states are now banning forfeitures before conviction. The federal government continues to use them.

Needless to say, the 5th Amendment grants us extremely important rights, most notably the right to not incriminate ourselves and the right to due process. These are cornerstones of our criminal legal system and are vigorously protected by criminal defense lawyers. *As I said earlier, the defense lawyers are the only protection we have from the absolutist rule of government.*

Sixth Amendment

"In all criminal prosecutions, the accused shall enjoy the right to a speedy and public trial, by an impartial jury of the State and district wherein the crime shall have been committed, which district shall have been previously ascertained by law, and to be informed of the nature and cause of the accusation; to be confronted

> *with the witnesses against him; to have compulsory process for obtaining witnesses in his favor, and to have the assistance of counsel for his defense."*

A much litigated Amendment, let's consider it one subject at a time.

First is the right to a speedy trial. The person accused of a crime, the defendant, has the right to a speedy trial. The length of 'speedy' is subject to interpretation, and varies in different jurisdictions, but it is an absolute right. The defendant can waive the right to a speedy trial, which often takes place when the case is complicated and his counsel needs additional time to prepare. But the prosecution has no right to waive the right to a speedy trial. The right belongs to the defendant alone. If the defendant does not waive the right to a speedy trial, and the prosecution is not prepared to go forward with the trial by the deadline, then the case must be dismissed and the defendant must, if in custody, be freed. In addition, with rare exceptions, the trial is to be public. The most notable exception is trials where a juvenile is the defendant. An adult defendant can ask that his trial be private but only under rare circumstances which the judge must approve. There is no inherent right to waive a public trial.

The defendant has the right to be tried by a jury of his peers. The defendant can waive his right to a jury and let the judge determine his guilt or innocence, but the prosecution can also demand a jury. In civil cases, either side may demand a trial by jury which is binding on the other party.

A defendant has the right to know, when he is arraigned on the charges, exactly what the charges are. The defendant has an absolute right to see any exculpatory evidence in the possession of the police or the prosecutor. The defendant also has the right to see all of the evidence against him. Though these rights have often been violated by the withholding of evidence, when it is later proven that exculpatory evidence was withheld by the state, a reversal of the conviction, or a mistrial, is almost automatic.

The 6th Amendment also provides that a defendant may ask the court to issue subpoenas for witnesses that are favorable to the defendant but who have refused or are reluctant to appear in court and testify. On occasion, because these witnesses are reluctant to come to court voluntarily, defense counsel will ask that the witness be deemed a 'hostile witness', and therefore, counsel is allowed to cross- examine the witness. And of course, the prosecution also has the right to cross-examine these witnesses. Which brings us to the right of confrontation, or the right to cross-examine, any witness. It has often been said that cross-examination is the greatest tool available to ascertain the truth, and that is a fact. An effective cross-examination may reveal information that is being concealed, undermine the credibility of a witness, challenge a witness' memory, and so on. Many trials turn on the results of cross-examination, and therefore it is the most important tool in the lawyer's arsenal. It is also the most difficult trial skill to learn, and it is definitely a learned skill. Other than direct experience cross-examining witnesses, the best thing that a young or inexperienced lawyer can do is to sit and watch a good cross-examiner at work.

And finally, but of great importance, the 6th Amendment guarantees the right to be represented by counsel. This is so ingrained in our system, and such a fundamental right, that it is included in the Miranda warnings. The accused must be advised of his right to counsel before he can be questioned. And the accused has the right to be represented, and be advised by, counsel at every step of the proceedings. In the event that you cannot afford to hire a lawyer, the government is required to provide a lawyer for you. The Supreme Court has ruled that an appointed lawyer, as well as a private lawyer, must give you representation that is both competent and effective.

The effectiveness of counsel is often the subject of appeals and often the first claim that a convicted defendant makes on appeal. Many effective lawyers have been challenged as ineffective for the purposes of appeal. And in capital crimes, punishable by life in prison or death, the effectiveness of counsel is always used as an argument. But its interpretation has its aberrations. The Texas Supreme Court, for example, has upheld convictions, ruling that counsel who fell asleep or were drunk, still offered effective assistance. Hard to believe; astonishing to hear; but true.

Seventh Amendment

"In suits at common law, where the value in controversy shall exceed twenty dollars, the right of trial by jury shall be preserved, and no fact tried by a jury shall be otherwise reexamined in any court of the United States, than according to the rules of the common law."

This Amendment has never been changed. It stands as it did in 18th century colonial America when twenty dollars was a lot of money. It is still the law of the land. But try getting a jury in a small claims case that involves $20. Or $1,000. Or $2,000. Or explain the rule of many states that a civil case that does not exceed a certain threshold amount must go to binding arbitration rather than to a trial. There is no right to a jury in any of these instances. Now I agree with every one of you that we should not be holding jury trials over a $20 dispute but is it worth a constitutional amendment?

The second part of the Amendment is far more important. When a jury, or a judge when a jury is waived, determines a fact to be true, no appeals court is allowed to reexamine the evidence and come to a different conclusion. The Appeals Court can decide that the facts of the case do not warrant the verdict, or that a certain fact should have been excluded under the rules of evidence, but they cannot change the 'fact' itself. This amendment also means that different courts cannot reach different results on a 'fact', a concept called res adjudicate. Once a fact is determined, it must be taken as previously established. This prevents conflicting rulings by different courts, and discourages forum shopping, which is the practice of looking for the court which the lawyer believes will be the most favorable.

Eighth Amendment

"Excessive bail shall not be required, nor excessive fines imposed, nor cruel and unusual punishments inflicted."

A large minority in our society, in modern times, has come to question whether the death penalty constitutes cruel and unusual punishment. How can a moral society, one of laws, condone murder by government when it condemns murder by individuals? Others have argued that specific means of the death penalty are cruel and unusual because the condemned person suffers for a period of time as they are put to death. They are now even arguing about which chemicals, and from which sources, can be used for lethal injection. In most states which do not have the death penalty, the automatic sentence for a capital offense is life in prison without possibility of parole.

Before moving on to further discussion of cruel and unusual punishment, let me stake out my own position on this. I believe in the death penalty when there is no doubt that the condemned person is guilty. Fortunately, with the advent of DNA testing, we can now know with far greater certainty when an innocent person has been sentenced to death. We can also know, with almost as much certainty, when a guilty person has been rightfully convicted.

I believe that the debate over which chemicals is the least painful during lethal injection is ludicrous. I believe that avoiding any discomfort or....gasp!....pain for the person being executed is ridiculous. How many of their victims suffered as little pain as we are trying to give to their killers, rapists, and kidnappers? I do not care if people who are hanged strangle slowly rather than having their necks immediately broken. I do not care if people in a gas chamber suffer in extreme pain as they are dying. I do not care if a prisoner shot by a firing squad continues to live in pain for a few more minutes.

But I care passionately that we only punish the truly guilty. While in law school, I read a book that told the stories of one hundred innocent men and women who were put to death and who were later proven, beyond doubt, to be innocent. And this long before the advent of DNA testing or any modern science, such as ballistics, was commonly used in trials. So be sure to honor the presumption of 'innocent until proven guilty', train prosecutors to seek truth rather than convictions, and use every means possible to prove the innocence of an individual.

Other methods of cruel and unusual punishment that have been debated over the years are the life sentence without possibility of parole (aren't we supposed to rehabilitate prisoners?), physical torture or the infliction of pain (whippings, use of electricity during questioning, keel-hauling, waterboarding, and the like).

On the subject of 'excessive bail', the courts have repeatedly ruled that the purpose of bail is to ensure that people attend their scheduled court dates. If you are deemed a flight risk, then bail will be set higher or denied completely. Factors taken into account include whether you have previously missed court dates, your ties to the community, family, employment, etc. Of course, some people are denied bail, or have a bail set so high that the judge knows they cannot meet it. Sometimes they are held because they pose a continuing threat to society, or to potential witnesses, or are in personal danger themselves. Who would argue that Bernie Madoff would not have fled the country if given the chance? Or that Casey Anthony was in personal danger from people who prejudged her? Or that O. J. Simpson was not a flight risk? Wait a minute, there was that slow moving, nationally televised, car chase around Los Angeles.... isn't there another law that requires a minimum speed on highways?

But in general, bail is granted and set at a reasonable amount. Society has no legitimate interest, and no right, to imprison people who will be exonerated at trial.

Ninth Amendment

"The enumeration in the Constitution, of certain rights, shall not be construed to deny or disparage others retained by the people".

Very simply stated, this amendment only provides that if a specific right, freedom or liberty is not specifically granted to – or protected for - people in the constitution that does not entitle any government to deny other rights which are inherent to the people. This amendment is rarely litigated.

Tenth Amendment

"The powers not delegated to the United States by the Constitution, nor prohibited by it to the states, are reserved to the States respectively, or to the people."

This is the 'states rights' amendment because it ensures that any powers not specifically granted to the federal government, or prohibited to the states, by the constitution, specifically belong to the states or to the people. It provides for two essential things. First, it is an explicit statement of the nature of government conceived by the authors of the constitution: that the federal government shall be limited in scope and only concerned with matters that affect the nation as a whole. Second, it reiterates that the rights given to individuals in the Bill of Rights belong to the people and cannot be taken away, diminished or modified by actions of any government.

Those numerous and valuable rights, which define our liberty and our status as the greatest and most free nation on earth, can only be taken away by another amendment to the constitution. Or by activist judges with a revisionist view of the constitution.

Yes, I know that there are those that disagree with me on the unqualified right to free speech in the 1st Amendment, there are those who would censor some parts of the press and other writings, and there are those who would argue that large peaceful assemblies and protests should not be allowed because they are 'inconvenient' or violate the opinion of others. But those rights are essential to a free society. And there are those who disagree with me and would put limitations on the rights of gun owners, including those who would ban individual gun ownership altogether. Writer's Note: In Mexico, individual ownership of guns is strictly illegal and carries a minimum prison sentence of one year. And in Mexico, over the last four years, there have been more than 40,000 murders due largely to cartel violence and terrorism. How many of those deaths would have been avoided, particularly the civilian deaths, if Mexicans were allowed to defend themselves as Americans are?

And there are those who would argue that arrestees have no rights that should be read to them, no right to free counsel, no right to inconvenience others by demanding a jury trial, and no right to not incriminate themselves. And that none of us should be able to refuse an unlawful police entry into our homes, our cars, and our persons. But these are the bedrocks which protect us, and which make us safer and unique in the world.

Yes, there will always be exceptions and violations. Police will lie about their right to search a house, will walk without consent through the house when granted only entrance to the front door, will lie during interrogations (very often telling suspects that they really do not need a lawyer), and other such violations. Because we are flawed as people, we cannot hope to make enforcement of the laws perfect. We can only do our best.

And remember that the Bill of Rights is subject to adjudication by the courts, with whom the final interpretation resides. And their interpretation has caused innumerable exceptions and contradictions over the years. But what are they if not human beings too?

Fourteenth Amendment

"Section. 1. All persons born or naturalized in the United States and subject to the jurisdiction thereof, are citizens of the United States and of the State wherein they reside. No state shall make or enforce any law which shall abridge the privileges or immunities of citizens of the United States; nor shall any State deprive and person of life, liberty, or property, without due process of law; nor deny to any person within its jurisdiction the equal protection of the laws.

Section, 2. Intentionally omitted.

Section. 3. Intentionally omitted.

Section. 4. The validity of the public debt of the United States, authorized by law, including debts for payment of pensions and bounties for services in suppressing insurrection or rebellion, shall not be questioned. But neither the United States nor any State shall assume or pay any debt or obligation incurred in aid of insurrection or rebellion against the United States, or any claim for the loss or emancipation of any slave; but all such debts, obligations and claims shall be held illegal and void.

> **Section. 5. The Congress shall have power to enforce, by appropriate legislation, the provisions of this article."**

Having referred to the 14th Amendment before, let me say that it is, by far, one of the most important Amendments to the Constitution.

First, let me explain why I have omitted Sections 2 and 3: they are of relatively little importance compared to the three provisions of this amendment that impact Americans in a huge way. Section 2 is simply concerned with the apportionment of seats in the House of Representatives based upon the population of the states. Section 3 simply states that no person who, having previously taken an oath to support the Constitution, as a member of the federal or state governments, engages in insurrection or rebellion against the United States (or a state), or given aid or comfort to the enemies of the country, shall be qualified to hold federal, state or local office again. Except, oddly enough, that Congress may 'remove such disability' by a two-thirds vote.

Now the three things that really matter in the 14th Amendment: the applicability of the Bill of Rights to the states, the equal protection clause, and the issue of public debts and pensions.

The 14th Amendment is best known and utilized, particularly by trial lawyers, because it provides that no state (and therefore any lesser level of government) shall make any law which 'abridges the privileges or immunities of citizens of the United States'. Thus, the Bill of Rights, which includes all of those vital and necessary rights, privileges and liberties which we have previously discussed, are binding upon the states and not just the federal government. Prior to the 1867 passage of the 14th Amendment, the Bill of Rights only applied to the federal government. After its passage, the lesser governments also became bound to honor and not abridge those same rights. This has huge and positive implications for all citizens of the United States because it means that we are protected against encroachment of our lives by governments of all sizes. It is also, for that reason, the source of most constitutional litigation. It comes into play in every arrest, investigation or criminal prosecution. It comes into play with our virtually unfettered right of free speech and freedom of the press. It comes into play with protests and rallies. The bottom line is that we are protected from the self-assumed authority of governments, in many ways, that allow our American way of life to be as it is.

The second part of Section 1 that is of great importance, and also the source of much controversy and litigation, is the provision requiring due process and requiring that all people be given equal protection under the law. This has led to various laws such as voting rights, attempts to prevent racial or religious discrimination, and affirmative action requirements in employment, schools and universities, the military, and governments. It is a difficult amendment to enforce, and has led to backlashes (such as reverse discrimination), but in the whole, it is a crucial requirement in an America in which we are all told that 'anyone can be president'.

Let's move to Section 4 of the 14th Amendment. It states that *'The validity of the public debt of the United States, authorized by law, including debts incurred for payment of pensions....shall not be questioned'*. We saw the importance of this constitutional mandate in 2010, when the country was teetering on the brink of defaulting on our public debt and Barack Obama was threatening that social security checks might not be issued. No politician in Washington was discussing this issue, as the president and congress played their idiotic game of brinkmanship, but the fact is that the constitution already mandated the result. Yet did you hear about it in the media, from the talking heads of our twenty-four hour news, of from any politician's office? The answer is "No". The United States is prohibited from not paying its public debt, which is at least the interest on loans that the government has taken from foreign nations and investors, as well as the interest on treasury issued bonds and bills. In fact, the government would be prohibited from not redeeming any such debts when they are mature and the owners or investors demanded payment of the debt. But even more interesting is that the President Obama threatened publicly that social security checks might not be issued if Congress did not break its deadlock on the government debt and possible default. This clause in the 14th Amendment requires that the president order the secretary of the treasury to make timely and full payments on the public debt, and that all pensions be paid, which includes both social security and civil service pensions. That the president was using this threat to frighten and intimidate American citizens is difficult to accept and clearly unconstitutional because it was a clear statement that if congress did not act, the president intended to abrogate his oath to uphold the Constitution by allowing the public debt and pensions to be questioned, as in 'not paid'. Fortunately, this scenario was narrowly avoided by congress with a bill to increase the debt ceiling, but which was only good for a matter of weeks. Subsequent increases in the debt ceiling averted the crisis. But only temporarily. We continue to wrestle with this issue and, it is fair to assume, that the president still believes he has the power to ignore the 14th Amendment. If that does come to pass, it will likely be the greatest constitutional crisis since the Civil War.

The Amendments That Were Left Out

During the debate in Congress over the ten amendments that did pass, and became the Bill of Rights, there were a few more ideas and amendments that were proposed but rejected.

The first was an idea that later was incorporated in the 27th Amendment, which was added in 1992. It restricts Congress' ability to change its own pay while in session.

The second was proposed by James Madison in which he wanted the states to have a) equal rights of conscience, b) freedom of the press, and c) mandatory trial by jury in criminal cases. As discussed earlier, the 14th Amendment, in 1867, made the first ten amendments applicable to the states and so Madison's desire for freedom of the press and right to a jury trial in criminal cases were eventually binding upon the states. But his desire for an equal right to conscience, whatever he intended by that, is not a part of the constitution. Perhaps it is better left to individual morality.

The third was an amendment to delineate the clear and distinct roles for each part of government but that was rejected because the body of the constitution already included a sufficient, though concise, explanation of the three parts of government.

Madison also argued that the first ten amendments should be included in the body of the Constitution but that was rejected for two reasons. First, the constitution was still a very new and untested document and the delegates feared that changing it and requiring its passage, in its entirety, by states for a second time would cause the document to fail, leaving the fledgling country without a governing document. That risk was too great to consider. The second reason was that the constitution contained a mechanism for it to be amended which required ratification by congress (2/3 of both houses) and three quarters (3/4) of the states. It was believed that incorporating the freedoms of the Bill of Rights by amending the constitution was a safer route. As it turns out, the delegates were right and the first ten amendments were adopted very quickly.

Finally, there was an effort to include a conscientious objector provision in the Second Amendment. It would have read *"but no person religiously scrupulous of bearing arms shall be compelled to render military service in person"*. It was many, many years before any right of religious or morally conscientious objection was recognized. America's most famous conscientious objector, Cassius Clay, later known to the world as Muhammad Ali, served time in federal prison when he refused to be drafted during the early years of the Vietnam War. But that never deterred many young men, who desiring to not serve in the military, found ways around it. And during the Civil War, young men were allowed to hire a surrogate to answer the draft and to serve in their stead.

CHAPTER TEN

Interesting, Strange…and True!

There are times when a case or claim arises, or an event happens in court, which is unique and often defies explanation. Lawyers scratch their heads in puzzlement at judges' rulings, observers become confused as to what they just witnessed, and institutions that are highly regarded often commit inexplicable acts that hurt their own members. This chapter gives an overview of times when the law and justice collide. Sometimes it works out; often it does not. So indulge me while I tell a few stories.

Being Sued For Money You Do Not Owe

Years ago, a client whom I had represented for years contacted me. I was general counsel for his company that built manufactured homes, we were involved in dozens of real estate transactions together, and I helped him, directly or indirectly, with several other problems. He was a self-made man: a Horatio Alger story of American success. Born into a working class family in a suburb of Boston, he was very hard working and had a strong desire to succeed. He was not educated beyond high school, but he had inherited his parents' strong work ethic and desire to succeed in their new country.

Nothing mattered more than his family and watching his sons succeed. When he was at the height of success, a multi-millionaire, he bought his sons a country club and thus ensured their livelihood and their prosperity for life. Through the years, he built hundreds of houses, developed subdivisions, built strip malls, and when I was introduced to him, he had just purchased his manufactured housing company. Everything was working in his life.

His next project involved a commercial property that Nick, along with three friends, intended to develop into an office building. They secured the construction financing at a local bank, and the project took off. Sometime later, Nick decided that he wanted to withdraw from the project, so they all returned to the same bank, which agreed that it would continue the loan – the construction financing – without Nick's involvement. New loan and mortgage documents were prepared, and Nick was not included. He was released from the debt. He signed nothing for the bank in that second transaction. It is important to remember that there were now two sets of loan documents issued and approved by the same bank, one which included Nick and the second set that did not include him.

Some history is necessary. In the great depression of the 1930's, banks both large and small were failing on a regular basis. Although they had become insolvent, the banks still had assets, often in the form of outstanding loans that they were owed or real estate upon which they had already foreclosed. The federal government created a corporation known as the Resolution Trust Company, which had the mandate to liquidate the banks that failed and which the government had taken over. The idea was a good one: collect the assets of the failed banks.

Bankers knew they were subject to federal or state audits, sometimes scheduled and sometimes without prior notice. So a practice developed in which the bankers would ask their friends for help. The friend would sign a promissory note that was fraudulent in that no money changed hands, and the banker promised his friend that the bank would never attempt to collect the loan. It was a fake. Why? Because a promissory note - proof of an outstanding loan - was an asset for the bank, and as long as the auditors agreed that the bank was solvent, it would remain open. Many banks were successful in deceiving the auditors with this type of fraud.

One bank that failed held a valid promissory note issued by a French company known as D'oench Dhume & Co., Inc. The dispute over collection of the note was largely a dispute over which state had jurisdiction over the bank and the claim, but in its ruling the U.S. Supreme Court also announced a doctrine which states that any fraudulent notes were collectible, and the only way for a borrower to disprove liability was actual proof from the bank that the loan had been paid in full. A canceled promissory note, a letter from the bank acknowledging that the note was paid, or a canceled check or receipt was required. No other proof was acceptable.

What became known as the D'oench Dhume doctrine applied only to outstanding promissory notes that Resolution Trust was trying to collect. To this day, that doctrine, set forth in 1942, remains the law. See 315 U.S. 447 (1942) for the full decision. In the recession that hit many parts of the country in the early 1990's, Resolution Trust was again very active in collecting the assets of failed banks.

In the recession, Nick lost his manufacturing company and all of the money that he had invested in the company as well as many other properties. Nearing retirement, he had nothing left but his house and cars. Even the country club was gone.

And then the small bank that Nick and his former partners used also failed.

It is crucial to remember that when the bank failed, Nick owed them nothing. The bank's records, then and forever in the possession of Resolution Trust, proved that conclusively.

Resolution Trust entered the picture, and seeing a large loan secured by partially developed real estate, rubbed its governmental hands in glee. Resolution Trust hired two large law firms, one in Texas and one in New York, to collect a promissory note in Boston. There are many competent lawyers who can handle a collection case in Boston, but for unknown reasons, Resolution Trust hired two out of state law firms. The law firms were given carte-blanche to handle the case as they saw fit. They filed their lawsuit in the U.S. District Court in Boston. Nick asked me to represent him, and I agreed. It developed into a jaw dropping experience in governmental over reach and judicial arrogance, the likes of which I had never seen.

Several times per week, I would receive Federal Express boxes filled with discovery requests, disclosures, hundreds of pages of exhibits and evidence, motions, and every other document or pleading that the law firms could create. Most of the documents that I received were exactly the same as documents that I received from the other law firm a few days before or later. Both Nick and I were in a state of disbelief. Why two law firms? Why were they out of state? Why were we being deluged with unnecessary and repetitive documents? What was all of this costing Resolution Trust, and the Federal government, and finally, the borrowers, who would be ordered to pay the attorneys' fees and expenses? Although some of the answers were clear, others were not. Again, why two law firms? Because they were both in Resolution Trust's good graces and received much of its national business. Why more than one lawyer at each law firm? Because it increased the firm's billable hours. Why were they out of state? Again, because both were in Resolutions Trust's good graces. Why were we deluged with so many documents? Same answer. The ultimate cost? It was not revealed by the time that I got Nick out of the case, but based on what I know about legal fees and all of the gouging techniques that were available and being used, the total cost to Resolution Trust could not have been less than $250,000.00. More likely, it was closer to $500,000.00. And don't forget, this was just a simple, no-brainer collection case. And from the very beginning, it was obvious that none of the defendants that signed the promissory note for several million dollars had any ability to pay it. It all depended on the success of the construction project. And that ended when Resolution Trust seized the bank.

When Nick was sued, Resolution Trust, and its law firms, knew that he owed nothing. But you know lawyers by now – they sue everyone in sight. Nick and I made a deliberate decision to not respond to the discovery, to not file any discovery requests, and to file no motions in court. It would have been an enormous waste of my time *and* Nick could no longer afford to pay large legal bills. And there was nothing to gain. So we did only the minimal work on the case: compliance with any court orders and attending any court hearing. It still cost him $10,000.00 even though he had no liability on the debt. Our legal system had already taught him when to fight and when to not fight.

Two weeks before the case was scheduled for jury trial (jury trials take much longer than trials before just a judge; hence, more legal fees), Judge William Young, who to this day is the most arrogant and self-righteous judge I ever encountered, and to whom the case was assigned, scheduled a conference in his chambers. Every lawyer was required to attend. First, he announced that he would allow only four days for the entire trial: Two days were to be given to Resolution Trust to prove that there was an unpaid promissory note and the identities of the people who signed it. They could do that in two hours. Two more days, in total, were allotted to the four men being sued. His clerk was to keep a time clock on her desk, and each of the defense lawyers was to be timed. We were allowed a maximum of four (4) hours to make an opening statement, make and argue any objections, cross-examine adverse witnesses, present our own case, and make our closing arguments. At the end of our four hours, we were forbidden to say another word. Frankly, I think that if the Supreme Court ever heard of that ruling, it would have been reversed by a unanimous vote. It was clearly a denial of due process and equal protection. And it was nothing more than an effort to give the government the upper hand, which it already had. That order was a slap in the face to the constitutionally guaranteed right of due process, which includes *"an opportunity to be heard"*.

But neither the facts nor the constitutional right of due process were going to defer the determined Judge Young. During the conference, he went around the room and asked each lawyer what his defense would be. When he reached me, he asked whom I represented and what defense I had. If I had any. I answered that my defense was quite simple: Nick had not signed the second note that was a bank asset when Resolution Trust failed and was therefore not liable. Judge Young immediately asked whether Nick had a canceled promissory note from the bank, a receipt showing payment, or a canceled check, I responded "No, the bank and now Resolution Trust have those records." Why would he, I asked, if he was not a party to the loan to the rewritten note? Judge Young immediately issued an order that forbade Nick from testifying that he was not liable on the note, forbade me from explaining to the jury the difference between the two notes, and forbade me from cross-examining Resolution Trust witnesses about the two notes. Further, I could not argue the matter to the jury. I was flabbergasted. Not only was he forbidding a valid defense, he was ordering that we could not provide crucial evidence to the jury. When I pointed out that there were two notes, and Nick had not signed the second one, on which he was being sued, Judge Young told me that he was following the Supreme Court's decision in D'oench Dhume. All fine and good, but that is not what the Supreme Court said in D'oench Dhume. Judge Young did not understand and misapplied the doctrine. It applied only to fraudulent transactions. Nick was not remotely involved in a fraudulent transaction. If a federal judge is going to issue such a draconian order, then he better know what the Supreme Court said. Judge Young did not know, did not care, and would not listen.

So there we were. No liability on the note and an order forbidding us from proving it. I could not explain it to Nick. It made no sense. For the better part of two weeks, I agonized over how to prove our case in the face of Judge Young's order. Two days before the trial, the answer came to me. I called the lead trial lawyer for Resolution Trust, who asked whether I was calling to offer a settlement. When I told him no, that I was calling to offer him an opportunity to drop Nick from the case, his laughed. When he stopped, he asked me why he should ever consider doing that. Here's what I said.

I reminded him that in order to prove his own case, he had to offer into evidence not only the first promissory note but the second one as well. The first one named Nick; the second one did not. I told him that, in compliance with Judge Young's order, I would make no opening statement, cross-examine no witnesses, make no objections, and offer no evidence. I would, however, reserve the right to make a closing argument to the jury. I explained to him that my closing argument would take only five minutes, and that I would not lose the case. Now his concern was growing rapidly. You see, all I planned to do was use his own evidence, show it to the jury, and ask them to carefully compare the names and signatures on the first note with the names and signatures on the second note. And then I would simply ask them *"How would you feel if you were sued on a promissory note that you did not sign?"* He caught on quickly, especially for a lawyer in a large firm. I had him trapped by his own evidence, and I was in full compliance with Judge Young's order. So I offered him a deal: If he would sign an agreement to dismiss Nick from the case, and if he did so before the case began, then we would go away silently. But if he did not sign before the case began, then I would refuse to sign such a agreement at any time, and I would make my simple point to the jury. When he hesitated, I asked him to consider why the government would sue a man whom the government knew was not responsible, and whether the jury would then begin to question the integrity of the government's case *and* its lawyers. He still did not agree; he wanted to think it over.

So two days later, we all showed up for the trial. I had the agreement to dismiss in my pocket, which I had already signed, and after we were seated I reached forward and handed it to him. As the bailiff called the jury in, he signed it and handed it back to me. I immediately walked to the front of the courtroom (which we were not allowed to do) and gave it to the judge's clerk, who immediately handed it to the judge (who, in an inappropriate display in front of the jury, was glowering at me). Judge Young read the three lines, signed it, and told us to leave. Nick had no idea what I had just done and looked at me with utter confusion when I signaled him to follow me. I told him to be quiet until we were out of the courthouse and several blocks away so that we could not be found. Only then did I explain it to Nick. The next day he came to my office unannounced and handed me a $5,000.00 bonus.

Don't you just love the fairness of our system and those government employees who administer it? Remember, judges are just government employees

The FBI and Four Innocent Men

In 2007, Federal Judge Nancy Gertner (a highly respected criminal defense lawyer in her own right) ordered the federal government to pay a record $101,750,000 to the families of two men who died in prison and to another two men who survived nearly thirty years in prison because FBI agents withheld evidence that would fully exonerate the four men. They were accused of killing Teddy Deegan, a small time hood, in 1965. Judge Gertner stated that FBI agents Dennis Condon and H. Paul Rico knew they could prove the four men were innocent, In addition, the two agents lied to state prosecutors, claiming that they had verified their informants' statements indicating the guilt of those men. The result was that four innocent men spent almost three decades (30 years!) in prison with the full knowledge and acquiescence of the FBI. And the reason for the lies?

The FBI agents wanted to protect the identities of their informants. As Judge Gertner stated, *"The FBI's misconduct was clearly the sole cause of this conviction"*, and that the government's position in opposing the award of damages *"is, in a word, absurd"*.

The End of the Attorney-Client Privilege?

A well-known liberal activist and defense attorney, Lynne Stewart, was sentenced to twenty-eight months in prison on her conviction for 'conspiracy and providing material support' to terrorists. She is known for representing controversial, poor, and unpopular defendants. Her case is disturbing for a number of reasons. The background: Ms. Stewart was the attorney for Sheik Omar Abdel-Rahman, an Egyptian cleric, who was serving a sentence in Colorado's federal super-max prison. In order to be able to see her client, she agreed to not pass messages from him to his supporters (a constitutionally dubious abuse of the attorney-client privilege). Whenever she visited him in prison, she was accompanied by an interpreter, as she did not speak Arabic and her client did not speak English. Therefore, any 'discussions' were spoken in Arabic and translated for her.

She was indicted for passing forbidden messages and conspiracy to do so. When she was convicted and sentenced to twenty-eight months, her statement to reporters was, *"I can do that standing on my head"*. Apparently, this was viewed by the appeals court as demonstrating a lack of remorse. Upon her felony conviction she was immediately disbarred in New York. Upon appeal, the federal appellate court ordered the trial judge to re-sentence her based upon her 'lack of remorse' and her 'alleged' perjury at her trial. But no defendant is ever required to show remorse, particularly when they believe they are innocent. And she was never charged with perjury. The appellate court simply ordered that she be re-sentenced. At her re-sentencing, the trial judge gave her ten years instead of twenty-eight months. At that time, she was seventy-one years old. It was possibly a life sentence.

So what is troublesome about this case? Several things. First and foremost, why were the prison authorities listening to and recording her conversations with her client? This is a clear invasion of the attorney-client privilege, which is one of the most sacred tenets of our legal system. No one can be presumed guilty and re-sentenced for 'allegedly' committing a crime. Either they are guilty of perjury, after a full and fair trial, or it is irrelevant. It is not within the appellate court's jurisdiction to even address the issue. So for the appellate court to order a re-sentencing for those two reasons defies the law and common sense, for it placed her in double jeopardy, which is expressly forbidden by the Constitution.

In sum, her right of free speech was denied to her, her client's attorney-client- privilege was violated, and she was re-sentenced for an issue that was not even before the appellate court. It was clearly a case of the government lining up against an unpopular and politically incorrect attorney in an effort to intimidate her and violate both her and her client's rights.

Those Fun Guys at the FBI.........Again!

In the mid to late 1800's, the Irish potato famine caused tens of thousands of Irishmen to emigrate from Ireland to America, settling primarily in New York and Boston. In Boston, they were segregated into an area known as South Boston, and even there, the Irish separated themselves into neighborhoods based upon their county of origin. The Irish immigrants suffered the same fate as many other ethnic groups. They were unwanted and faced the twin problems of poverty and unemployment, as well as systemic discrimination.

One of these families was the Bulger family. Among their many children, two would later arise to public fame. Although raised by the same parents in the same neighborhood, their career paths could not have been more disparate.

James was several years older than his brother William and, because he was so generous and friendly to the younger neighborhood children, he acquired the respect and authority which he so assiduously encouraged. At some point he acquired the nickname "Whitey', which he used for life. His younger brother, William, became 'Billy', by which he was known for life. So now we have Whitey and Billy, probably the two most powerful men to ever come from South Boston.

Whitey chose a life of crime. He started out with small non-violent crimes, such as larceny, car theft, loan sharking, etc. As a young man, he spent a few years in Alcatraz. But as his power and temper both grew, more and more people, in and outside of South Boston, grew to respect and fear him. He became the undisputed mob boss of South Boston. Whitey was very smart and very cautious. As his empire grew, he moved into illegal narcotics, enforcement beatings, extortion, kidnapping and murder. But he was never directly involved in the activities that he ordered; there were always layers of other people, or 'buffers', between him and the actual crime. The Boston police and the FBI knew who he was and what he was doing, but could never produce evidence linking him directly to any crime. And the people of South Boston would not cooperate with law-enforcement, due to their tight-knit ethnic background, and more importantly, fear of Whitey's retribution.

As he was rising to power, Whitey became friends and business partners with Steven 'The Rifleman' Flemmi, a known hit man and enforcer. Their public façade was one of unity, but Whitey was the undisputed head of his organization.

At about this time (1960's and 70's), J. Edgar Hoover ordered the FBI's Boston office to destroy the Boston mafia, by which he specifically meant the Italian Mafia headed by Gennaro Angiulo and Raymond Patriarca. In addition to the Italian Mafia, there was also a mob family known as the

Winter Hill Gang, headed by Howie Winter. Whitey and Flemmi were associates of the Winter Hill Gang. But Hoover's focus, myopic as it often was, was only the Italians.

So the FBI, in a loose and untrusting confederation with the Boston police, began the mission of destroying the Italian mafia. They needed a way to infiltrate the group, obtain evidence, make arrests, and obtain convictions. Enter Whitey, who saw this as a golden opportunity to remove a rival. Unbeknownst to anyone, Whitey became an FBI informant, the worst betrayal in any organized crime group. And his collaboration led to success. The Italian mafia was eliminated and its leaders sentenced to life terms.

Now the only problem was Howie Winter and his group. The two fought for years for turf and power, and again Whitey prevailed when Winter and several of his lieutenants and soldiers went off to serve their own life sentences, Now Whitey ruled the underworld of Boston, but he never lost the caution and discretion that kept him in power. Of course, having the FBI in his pocket helped immensely.

Let's digress to Whitey's younger brother Billy. Billy went to college, law school, and entered politics. He eventually rose to be the President of the Massachusetts Senate, arguably the state's most powerful politician. He ruled with an iron fist, apparently a family trait, but he also never lost touch with his political base: the people of South Boston. At the same time that Whitey was the most powerful gangster in the state, his brother was the most powerful politician in the state.

One particular FBI agent, John Connolly, was assigned to 'run' Whitey and Flemmi and did so for twenty years. However, Connolly went too far - much too far - and became an informant inside the FBI on behalf of Whitey. Connolly 'paid' his informants by tipping them in advance to police raids, traps, informants and pending indictments. The reports from Connolly to Washington were filled with stories of success, future plans, and so on. Connolly became an FBI icon because his work had been so successful.

For several years, Billy lived in a Boston suburb next door to John Connolly. Coincidence? It was not uncommon for Whitey and Flemmi to go to Connolly's house for dinner, and for Billy to walk across the backyard and join them. After dinner, Connolly's wife excused herself, Billy reportedly walked back home, and the three informants then had their discussions, which included gifts and cash for Connolly.

Eventually and inevitably, the house of cards came tumbling down. Flemmi surrendered himself to the FBI on several felony indictments and began informing on the extent of Connolly's involvement. Connolly became the target of an internal FBI investigation, was indicted for several felonies, including murder, and is presently serving 40 years in federal prison. When Whitey learned of almost fifty federal indictments pending against him, including nineteen murders, he and his long-time girlfriend, Catherine Grieg...simply disappeared. That was in 1985. It was not until June, 2011 that they were captured living a quiet life in Santa Monica, California. They were caught because the FBI began running TV ads in major cities looking for Ms. Grieg, and an astute neighbor recognized her. When arrested, Whitey and Catherine had $800,000 and a small arsenal in their modest apartment. He has been convicted of all of the murders and sentenced to life in prison without parole. Ms. Grieg was convicted of lesser charges related to their escape and sentenced to several years in prison.

After the tragedy of 9/11, Osama Bin Laden became #1 on the FBI's Ten Most Wanted list, bumping Whitey down to #2.

And the final interesting twist. Congress began an investigation into the entire Whitey/FBI debacle that lasted twenty years, including how the astounding corruption of John Connolly went so long without being noticed. Billy Bulger, still President of the Massachusetts Senate, was subpoenaed to testify before Congress. He repeatedly stated that he had no communication with Whitey since his disappearance and had no idea where he was. He also said that if he had known, he would not have divulged the information. That comment spelled the end of Billy's tenure as President of the Senate, but he was appointed President of the University of Massachusetts, where he remained until his retirement, still a beloved and respected figure in largely Irish Massachusetts.

CHAPTER ELEVEN

Secession, Nullification, and the Dept. of "Justice"

An American Hero vs. the Department of Justice

Jay Dobyns is a true American hero. Very few people have heard of him, unlike Chris Kyle, the American hero now known around the world. For twenty seven years, Jay Dobyns worked undercover as an agent for the federal Bureau of Alcohol, Tobacco and Firearms (ATF). He is the only agent to have successfully infiltrated the criminal empire of the Hell's Angels. After his identity was exposed and he successfully emerged from his undercover work, the danger to himself and his family worsened. But this time, it was at the hands of senior ATF agents and supervisors, as well as a cadre of lawyers from Eric Holder's Justice Department.

After being exposed as a government agent, there were numerous death threats against Mr. Dobyns, his wife, and his teenage daughter. The ATF gave him no protection. His house was burned to the ground but his wife and daughter, who were home alone, escaped unharmed. When Dobyns "blew the whistle" and let it be known that ATF had done nothing to protect his family from clearly serious and credible threats, the

ATF accused him of setting fire to his own house with his family inside. The criminal threats, from which he received no protection, included the murder of Dobyns either by a bullet or by injection with the HIV virus, the kidnap and torture of his daughter, and the videotaped gang rape of his wife. Trial testimony proved that these threats and plans were laid out in prison letters and confirmed by FBI and ATF investigations and interviews with prison informants. Contracts were solicited between the Hell's Angels, the Aryan Brotherhood and the notorious Salvadoran MS-13 gang to carry out the threats. Knowing of these threats, the federal government did nothing to protect the Dobyns family.

Dobyns sued the ATF. In August, 2014, that trial ended with a verdict in Dobyns' favor for $173,000. Two months later, in October 2014, federal Judge Francis Allegra, who had presided over the trial, vacated the judgment. He provided no explanation. Less than two months after that Judge Allegra reinstated the original verdict in Dobyns' favor and this time the Judge gave plenty of reasons. Succinctly stated: The Judge believed that Justice Department attorneys, who had fought against Dobyns' claim for compensation, had "committed fraud on the Court". How so?

First, in 2012, a Justice Department attorney named Valerie Bacon asked Thomas Atteberry, the special agent in charge of the ATF Phoenix office, and Carlos Canino, assistant special agent in charge of the Tucson office, not to reopen their investigation into the arson because the results of the investigation would hurt the government's defense against Dobyns' lawsuit. Both Atteberry and Canino were witnesses in the Dobyns lawsuit. The Judge did not learn of the DOJ effort to squelch the investigation until after the trial, which he considered concealment by the DOJ. To their credit, the two agents ignored the DOJ attorney and continued their investigation. The arson has never been solved.

Second, and more seriously, Christopher Trainor, an ATF internal affairs investigator, who compiled evidence against the ATF, testified to Judge Allegra after the trial that he had been threatened by an ATF attorney and witness as a result of his investigation into the ATF's actions against Dobyns. Trainor was told that if he testified his own career would face repercussions.

Fraud on the court is defined as conduct 1) by an officer of the court (attorney), that 2) is directed to the 'judicial machinery' itself, that 3) is intentionally false, willfully blind to the truth or is in reckless disregard for the truth, 4) that is a positive averment or is a concealment when the officer of the court is under a duty to disclose, and that 5) deceives the Court.

The effect of Judge Allegra's finding that the DOJ had committed fraud on the court was twofold. First, Dobyns' judgment was immediately reinstated and second, in a very rare move, seven DOJ attorneys were barred from any further participation in the case.

And Judge Allegra took one other unusual step. He made a direct report of his findings regarding DOJ's corruption to Attorney General Eric Holder. To date, the Attorney General has not responded publicly.

Can the States Secede From the United States?

Periodically, throughout our nation's history, disgruntled citizens of a state(s) talk about seceding from the federal union. The only time it happened was before and during the Civil War (which was fought not to abolish slavery, but to preserve the integrity of the union). After the Confederacy lost the war, all of the states that had seceded were admitted back into the Union. But the question remains: May a state lawfully – constitutionally - secede from the Union?

In 1781, the thirteen Colonies ratified the Articles of Confederation – the precursor to the Constitution. At that time, the colonies had, only five years earlier, declared their independence from the totalitarian monarchy of England. In 1781, the colonial delegates were scrupulous in guarding the independence of the colonies. The delegates were heavily influenced by the independent wording of the colonies' own constitutions, and they were very concerned about preserving the independent status of each colony.

When the Constitutional Convention met in 1787, after the Revolutionary War had been won, its purpose was to amend the Articles of Confederation into a national constitution. In fact, the Constitution that emerged was substantially different than the Articles. Because the delegates, and indeed the colonists generally, feared a centralized state and the possibility of tyranny, the idea of separation of powers was born. It became the framework of the new United States – a coequal three part government comprised of the executive, legislative and judicial branches. The system of checks and balances among the coequal branches was meant to ensure that the executive did not gain too much authority.

Just as importantly, the 10th Amendment explicitly states that the new national – federal – government has only those powers specifically given to it. All other powers were retained by the states. So the first truth about secession emerges: When the thirteen colonies were independent of England, and before they adopted the Articles of Confederation, and before they adopted the Constitution, they were independent political entities. The colonies did not surrender their right of independence from one another in either the Articles or the Constitution. Because they did not surrender their right of independent existence to the federal government, they retained the right of independence, and therefore, the right of secession.

There is nothing in the Constitution that allows or precludes secession of a state. The Constitution is silent as to whether the voluntary association of the states into a union may be changed by the voluntary disassociation of one or more of the states from that union. There is no power granted to the federal government to prevent or reverse secession. That said, secession is a right that the states implicitly retained in the 10th Amendment. The states' right to secede can only be taken away by amendment to the Constitution.

It is often said that Texas retained the right of secession in its constitution when it joined the Union. When Texas was admitted as a state, it was one of only two states that were previously recognized as sovereign independent republics (Hawaii is the other).

But that myth about Texas is just that – a bit of Texas folklore. There is nothing in the Texas state constitution about secession from the Union. Texas is no different than the other fifty states in regard to its right to secede.

The question then becomes: What effect did the Civil War have on the issue of secession? And the answer is: None.

The Civil War began as an argument over tariffs being imposed by the federal government on the southern states. By all accounts, the tariffs were economically crippling (Contrary to what we learned in grade school, the Civil War was not fought over slavery. It was economic. Most wars are.). The states that seceded from the Union formed their own national government. When the war ended, the southern states were compelled to rejoin the federal government and reaffirm their allegiance to the U. S. Constitution. So I ask this: if the states that did secede did not have the right to secede, why did they have to rejoin the Union? If they had no right to do so, then they never left the Union in the first place. A state cannot be readmitted if, by law, it never left. It's just common sense.

Lincoln led the North against the South primarily to preserve the Union. It was America's most horrendous war. Six hundred thousand (600,000) Americans died in four years of war – more than all of America's other wars combined. Three years after the war ended, the U. S. Supreme Court ruled in a case called: Texas vs. White 74 U.S. 700 (1869). It is often hailed as the definitive law against secession. It is not. The White case was a dispute over the ownership of federal bonds that were owned and sold by Texas during the period of its secession. The Court ultimately ruled that Texas had not seceded legally, and therefore the actions of the Texas government during secession were null and void. The issue was not over

Texas' right to secede but the Court took the opportunity to expound on that issue. And they can't be blamed for grasping at the opportunity. The war had just ended and the southern states were, in a draconian manner, being forced to seek "readmission". The Court's decision was written by Chief Justice Salmon Chase, a member of Lincoln's cabinet and a leading Union figure. What else could the Court have done? To declare that the Civil War was pointless? To declare that 600,000 people died in vain? Neither of these ideas was politically or ideologically possible. The mood of the times required a determination that the confederate states were outlaws; that their succession was unconstitutional, if not treasonous. Chase's opinion is as convoluted a piece of legal reasoning as the Supreme Court has ever produced. It concluded that the history of the Constitution precluded lawful secession. But there was no such history and there were no documents to substantiate their conclusion. The Court created a "history" out of thin air.

Two years after Chase wrote of a constitutional history that precludes secession, President Ulysses Grant signed an act entitling Texas to representation in Congress, thus "readmitting" Texas to the Union. Again, Texas would not be readmitted if it never legally left in the first place.

These two events cannot be reconciled. Either secession was impossible and the Confederate states never left the Union, or secession was possible and the states had to be readmitted to the Union. Grant was right: the Confederate states had left the Union to form a different country and, thus, had to be readmitted. That contradiction has never been resolved but the secession deniers can't explain the contradiction.

White purports to stand for the notion that the Union is indivisible and that a state's allegiance to the Union is eternal. It is a flawed piece of legal reasoning in a case (about ownership of bonds) that should never have addressed secession. If anything, White muddied the waters of a clear pond.

All of which brings us to the contemporary questions. Should a disgruntled state secede? Will a state benefit by seceding? Of the fifty states, California and Texas are the two that have the best chance of survival as independent nations. California is the world's 12th largest economy. Texas is the world's 25th largest economy. Both have international seaports and international borders. Both have a strong and independent identity. But I believe that neither state, nor any state, would be best served by secession. I believe that the United States would be weakened by the secession of any state. And I predict that if any state does vote to secede, the reaction of the Union will be, as the Civil War taught us, immediate and violent.

The Moonlight Fire

The Moonlight Fire began on September 3, 2007 in Lassen County, California, a remote area near the Nevada border. It was a human caused fire on private land. Strong winds pushed smoke in all directions, eventually affecting the Sacramento Valley and the San Francisco bay area in California, as well as parts of Nevada and Utah. By the time the fire was fully contained sixteen days later, it had spread into the Plumas National Forest and burned a total of 65,000 acres. By any measure, it was a tragedy.

The cause of the fire remains undetermined. Initially, an employee of the logging contractor hired to clear the timber was blamed for causing the fire. Both federal and state officials accused Sierra Pacific Industries, a logging and paper company, of negligence in its hiring and supervision of the logging contractor. A California state judge ruled that the state could not prove its case, but a federal judge ruled that Sierra Pacific could be found liable even if its contractor did not cause the fire. After the federal ruling, Sierra Pacific, its contractor, and the owners of the land settled the case with a total payment of $55,000,000 and the transfer of 22,500 acres of land to the government in compensation for the loss of public forest and firefighting costs.

Later, the battle over responsibility for the fire became incendiary. Charges of corruption and cover-up were made against both California and federal officials involved in the investigation of the fire and the prosecution for its responsibility.

Before the fire was even put out, public officials decided that Sierra Pacific was liable for the fire, concluding that a bulldozer blade threw off sparks when it struck a rock.

After Sierra Pacific had paid a portion of the settlement, it petitioned the federal court to vacate the settlement due to fraud perpetrated upon the court by state and federal officials with the full knowledge and complicity of the government's lawyers. This began a series of revelations that once again highlighted the corruption in Eric Holder's Justice Department.

Sierra Pacific contended that federal prosecutors stood by during pretrial depositions, and knowing that it was false, allowed CA Dept. of Forestry Protection investigators and U. S. Forest Service investigators to "repeatedly lie under oath about the very foundation of their investigation". One of the documents filed with the Court is an affidavit from a former assistant U. S. attorney, E. Robert Wright, who swears that he was forced to give up his position as the government's lead lawyer on the case because he rejected pressure from a superior in the Justice Dept. "to engage in unethical conduct as a lawyer". There were instances when Mr. Wright sought advice of DOJ's office of professional responsibility, and in each instance, the office and Mr. Wright agreed that a lawyer has a duty both to disclose information and a duty to not misrepresent information, particularly by omission. Another former DOJ attorney, Eric Overby, was also removed from the case for refusing to engage in unethical and fraudulent behavior. He commented, "It's called the Department of Justice. It's not called the Department of Revenue" in a reference to the stated DOJ goal of collecting money from the defendants, apparently without regard to the truth or any respect for the integrity of the courts. Sierra Pacific insisted that the investigators' origin-and-cause report is a fraudulent document that distorts and even omits all information that could hurt the government's claim against Sierra Pacific. Specifically, the report blamed the bulldozer and sparks and omitted that investigators had originally concluded that the fire started at another location.

Sierra Pacific's position was bolstered when a Plumas, CA county judge, Leslie C. Nichols, ruled that Cal Fire was guilty of "egregious and reprehensible conduct" in investigating the fire and ordered it to pay $32,000,000 in damages to Sierra Pacific and the other defendants. The judge ruled that Cal Fire withheld documents, destroyed evidence and "engage in a systematic campaign of misdirection with the purpose of recovering money" from Sierra Pacific.

On the federal side, Judge Morrison C. England, Jr. was so incensed by the illegal conduct of the DOJ that he ordered the recusal of every federal judge in the district because the court had been defrauded by the federal government. However, the Chief Judge of the district rescinded that order. The final outcome is yet to be determined. But it's refreshing that judges in both the state and federal courts are standing against the corruption of both state and federal prosecutors when they perpetrate fraud upon the courts. It's time that Barack Obama's Justice Department be held accountable for its constant and ongoing unlawful activities.

Jury Nullification

Jury nullification is the decision by a jury to ignore the law, the facts, or both to render a verdict contrary to the law or the facts. It is limited almost exclusively to criminal cases but can also occur in civil cases.

Nullification is actually a right that belongs to each individual juror but it is most effective when invoked as a group. But nullification can occur when one juror prevents a criminal conviction, or prevents imposition of a death sentence. It can also prevent an acquittal, resulting in a hung jury.

There is a constitutional basis for nullification. It is found in several provisions. First, the requirement that juries render a general verdict in criminal cases, ie: guilty or not guilty, without reporting on specific facts or conclusions. Second is the inability of a judge to direct a specific verdict regardless of the strength of the evidence for either guilt or acquittal. Third is the prohibition against double jeopardy, in that a defendant cannot be retried for a crime for which they have been acquitted, and finally, the fact that a juror can never be punished for their decision in a case.

Jury nullification was first reported in America in 1670 when Quakers were acquitted by a jury of violating a law which permitted religious assemblies of only certain religions. This was unusual in that Quakers were often persecuted in colonial America for rejecting the Church of England. In 1735, John Zenger, a journalist was acquitted of the crime of publishing criticism of the Governor of the New York colony. Subsequent colonial juries acquitted defendants of violating England's Navigation Acts, which mandated that all colonial shipping pass through England for it to be taxed. Prior to and during the Civil War northern juries acquitted abolitionists for violating the Fugitive Slave Act because the jurors believed slavery to be unjust. Nullification of alcohol crimes during Prohibition is credited with giving impetus to the 21st Amendment, which repealed Prohibition. During the civil rights era of the mid-20th century, white juries acquitted white defendants accused of murdering blacks. Some argue that this was not a problem of jury nullification, but of jury selection, but that ignores the obvious fact that only whites could serve on juries. During the Vietnam War period, several defendants were acquitted of anti-war crimes and protests because sympathetic judges instructed the juries that they could follow their conscience.

Other notable examples of nullification are said to include Marion Barry, the former mayor of Washington DC for drug use, Lorena Bobbitt, who famously cut off her husband's penis as revenge for being regularly abused, and of course, O.J. Simpson. I do not agree that Simpson benefitted from nullification; I believe that he was acquitted as a result of the incompetence of the prosecutors and the trial judge.

Arguments for jury nullification focus on the precise language of the instructions given to jurors regarding the burden of proof. The instructions state that a defendant must be found not guilty if the case has not been proven beyond a reasonable doubt and should be found guilty if the case has been proven to that standard. The 'must' vs. 'should' dichotomy leaves a lot of room for a jury to exercise its discretion.

Should judges advise the jury that it has the right to decide what law to apply to the case – the right to nullify? And do judges advise juries of that right? In the 1794 case of Georgia vs. Brailsford, Chief Justice John Jay, speaking for a unanimous court, said,

> "It may not be amiss, here, Gentlemen, to remind you of the good old rule, that on questions of fact, it is the province of the jury, on questions of law, it is the province of the court to decide. But it must be observed that by the same law, which recognizes this reasonable distribution of jurisdiction, you have nevertheless a right to take upon yourselves to judge of both, and to determine the law as well as the fact in controversy. On this, and on every other occasion, however, we have no doubt, you will pay that respect, which is due to the opinion of the court. For, as on the one hand, it is presumed, that juries are the best judges of facts; it is, on the other hand, presumable, that he court are the best judges of the law. **But still both objects are lawfully, within your power of discretion.**"

This was a ringing endorsement of a juror's right to decide the law coupled with a plea that jurors follow the wisdom and knowledge of the court in deciding what the law is.

This rule of law lasted for exactly one hundred and one (101) years until Justice John Marshall Harlan, in 1895, speaking for the Court in Sparf vs. U.S. (156 US 51), ruled that a trial judge has no responsibility to inform the jury of its right to nullify laws. And that remains the status of the law on nullification – that the right exists but the judge has no responsibility to tell the jury that they have the right. The same result was found in a federal decision in 1969, U.S. vs. Moylan (417 F2d 1002). It is contradictory to say that a jury has a right, and that a defendant has the right for the jury to be aware of it, but the court has no duty to advise the jury of its right. The 1972 case of U.S. vs Dougherty (473 F2d 1113) took it a step further and affirmed that the jury has the right to nullify but refused the defendant's request to inform the jury of its right. In 1988, in U. S. vs. Krzyske (857 F2d 1089), the jury specifically asked the judge if it could nullify and the judge told the jury that no such thing existed. The appeals court affirmed the right of nullification but deemed the judge's untrue instruction as being insignificant. The defendant was convicted. The U.S. Supreme Court is studiously silent on the subject.

There are numerous fallacies and myths about nullification and it is fun to consider them. One is that jury nullification undermines the rule of law. In truth, nullification allows jurors to follow their conscience when they believe a prosecution is unjust. And as we have discussed, nullification is the law. Certainly, jurors have used nullification to produce unjust results, such as in the Jim Crow south, when no white defendants were convicted of murdering black citizens, but the abuse of a right is not a reason to dissolve the right. Another is that the Supreme Court struck down jury nullification in 1894. But this is not true; the Court simply said that a judge was not required to inform a jury of the right. A third misconception is that nullification violates the juror's oath. This is simple to dispel: If a jury has the right to nullify, which they do, then it cannot be a violation of their oath to exercise their right. It is consistent with their oath. And finally, there are some who argue that juries will suspend good laws and convict the innocent. But studies show that juries rarely acquit a defendant who is clearly guilty and there is a victim of the crime. Acquittals in "victim crimes" are far more likely to occur when the police are not believed or the prosecution's case is just not strong enough to get beyond a reasonable doubt. O.J. Simpson is an example of both.

There are currently 3,200 prisoners in the United States serving life sentences without parole for non-violent offenses. The problem is that many of these people would be free, or convicted of much lesser offenses, had juries known of their right to determine the law to be applied and the right to vote their conscience.

CHAPTER TWELVE

"National Secrets and the 2&7/8 Government"

It began with an unremarkable, albeit tragic, crash of an Air Force plane in 1948, and ended with a constitutional crisis in which the Supreme Court abrogated part of its constitutionally mandated oversight of the presidency. Hence my statement that we now have a 2&7/8 part government. It is no longer a three-part government because the Supreme Court has made itself subservient to the presidency in a vital part of the Supreme Court's duties: oversight of national security matters.

Within one year after World War II ended, in July, 1945, the Cold War began. Rumors of a massive Soviet espionage ring operating in Washington were rampant. The Communist hysteria began in America. Russia continued to flex its military might as it took control of East Germany, half of Berlin, and began to annex the countries of Eastern Europe, which quickly had new Communist governments but were, in reality, governed by Moscow. A huge Russian military buildup began throughout Eastern Europe. The response in the American government was a near panic-stricken belief that Russia intended to annex all of Western Europe, not unlike the Nazis had done a few years earlier. The immediate American response was a massive troop build-up in Western Europe, particularly in West Germany, France, Italy and England. America's military might had been severely depleted by the end of World War II, so a race began between America and Russia to build up their military strength. At that time, only America had nuclear capabilities, but Russia soon developed its own nuclear weapons. Bomb shelters were built and school children taught to hide under their desks in the event of a nuclear war. By 1949, the Red Scare had fully taken effect. Loyalty oaths began to take hold, the trials of alleged Communists began, and lists of suspected Communist sympathizers were compiled, with the total eventually exceeding one million Americans. American Communism was viewed as a national security issue. The Cold War was on, attendant with much political saber-rattling, and lasted more than forty years.

At this time, America's military experts realized that future warfare would be won not at sea, but in the skies. The military turned its attention to the development of long-range missiles capable of carrying warheads, both nuclear and conventional. A fierce rivalry ensued: The Army Ground Forces, the Army Air Forces, and the Naval Forces all wanted to take the lead in developing this program. The Army Air Forces seized the momentum by declaring that it already had a long-range guided missile which it would publicly demonstrate. It did not.

Then Project Banshee began: the effort to develop a long-range guided missile along with the communications and control technology necessary to ensure its success. A team was assigned to develop a computerized radar system that would guide the drone missiles to targets thousands of miles away. The team consisted of both civilian electronics engineers and military personnel. The Air Force plane designated for use to deliver these missiles was the B-29, a notoriously unreliable plane with a history of failed components, engine fires, maintenance flaws, scarcity of parts, and worst of all, fatal crashes. The development and testing of the missile technology was transferred to Robins Air Force Base near Macon, Georgia, which was the home of the 3150th Electronics Squadron, whose sole purpose was to install the radar equipment and do the necessary test flights. On October 6, 1948, a B-29 carrying both military personnel and civilian engineers left Macon enroute to Orlando, Florida and back, for the purpose of testing the Banshee system by turning control of the plane over to the system rather than the pilots. That is the flight that crashed (under manual control) on a farm near Waycross, Georgia on October 6, 1948. The remnants of the plane, including its four engines, were strewn over a two mile radius from the crash site. Of the thirteen men on board, only four survived. Nine perished.

Police and firemen soon arrived at the scene, as did military personnel. The entire area was cordoned off to the public, and military investigators swarmed in. All civilians were prohibited by military officers from entering the farm.

Immediately upon hitting the news, questions arose as to the purpose of the flight and why civilians were on board. The Air Force simply stated that the bomber was engaged in 'electronic research of different types of radar'. The military conducted its 'investigation' and entirely cleared the crash site within only four days. There was an initial and inadequate investigation. A second, and more comprehensive investigation, was conducted a few months later. Three days before its release, the Air Force Chief of Staff classified the report as 'secret', then the highest security classification. Certainly no civilian eyes were to see the report, although rumors were already circulating that the Air Force was covering up some of the facts about the crash. By March, 1949, it appeared that the fight to learn the truth had ended. In fact, it had just begun.

Given the state of politics in the country, few were willing to question the government. But three widows of the deceased men, Betty Palya, Patricia Reynolds and Phyllis Brauner did just that. They eventually convinced attorney Charles J. Biddle, of the Philadelphia law firm of

Drinker Biddle & Reath to accept their case and to do so on a contingent fee basis. The firm received $50 in advance.

Charles Biddle was born to wealth and privilege, with his family being one of the first to settle in Philadelphia. In World War I, he was a flying ace with eight confirmed kills to his credit. He was wounded and shot down behind enemy lines, crashed his plane between German and British lines, and survived each time. He was awarded the Distinguished Service Cross, the Purple Heart, the French Legion of Honor, the Croix de Guerre, and the Belgian Ordre de Leopold. He returned home a war hero. After the war he attended Princeton and Harvard School of Law. He joined a patrician law firm where he distinguished himself as a gentleman and a talented litigator with a 'full speed ahead' attitude. His clients were banks, insurance companies and corporations. But it was no mystery why he chose to represent three poor widows and sue the federal government: His love of planes and flying naturally led to his curiosity about the B-29 crash and the secrets behind it.

In June, 1949, in behalf of two of the widows, Biddle filed a lawsuit against the federal government under the recently enacted Federal Tort Claims Act, alleging that the crash and deaths of their husbands "were caused solely by the negligent and wrongful acts and omissions of the officers and employees" of the United States of America. He asked for $300,000. (equivalent now to $2,265,169.) for each of them. In September, Patricia Reynolds joined the lawsuit, and so the long case proceeded, three grieving widows and Charles Biddle against the enormity of the federal government.

As with all civil cases, it began its long, slow journey through the courts.

Depositions were taken, interrogatories were filed and requests for the production of documents were made. Appropriate motions were filed and heard.

On November 16, 1949, the Air Force officially ended the Banshee project, declaring that it had not been successful in producing adequate missile guiding radar, and also citing the unreliability of the B-29 as the carrier for the missiles that were envisioned. Six days later, the government filed its response to the lawsuit, denying any negligence or liability, which is the normal response to any claim. Nothing was yet out of the ordinary. The slow discovery process began with Charles Biddle submitting thirty interrogatories to the government (written questions to be fully answered in writing and under oath). He also requested a copy of the accident report prepared by the Air Force, the plane's records of mechanical condition and maintenance, the written statements of the surviving crew members, whether the plane had any prior engine trouble, and a thorough written account of what had transpired on the plane. It would be kind to describe the government's responses as vague and incomplete, and it flatly refused to provide copies of the written documents. With that, the lawsuit hit a brick wall. That refusal would precipitate more than forty years of litigation.

Because of the government's failure to produce the records, Biddle asked for an order compelling the government to produce the records. The government's response was a motion to quash Biddle's request, stating that the records were privileged data and therefore confidential. The case was assigned to the Honorable William H. Kirkpatrick, a highly regarded and respected jurist who also had a reputation for requiring wide-ranging and extensive discovery. He heard the competing requests on February 15, 1950, but did not issue his ruling until June 30, 1950. He ruled in favor of the three widows. Coincidentally, that was the same day on which President Truman authorized the United States to go to war in support of South Korea.

After the ruling, the Air Force still refused to turn the documents over to the Attorney General (oddly enough, the Air Force's own attorney). It is important to note that the plaintiffs were not seeking any type of military information; simply the records regarding the plane itself. Judge Kirkpatrick had rejected the government's claims of privilege and confidentiality, so the government prepared affidavits that were signed, under oath, by two highly influential people: Secretary of the Air Force Thomas Finletter and Judge Advocate General Reginald Harmon. In Harmon's Affidavit, he referred to "national security" secrets. In Finletter's Affidavit, he alluded to his privilege as Secretary of the Air Force to set appropriate regulations regarding privacy and stated that "the aircraft in question, together with the personnel on board, were engaged in a highly secret mission of the Air Force". In a subsequent hearing, the Court addressed the Cotton Valley Operators case, a U.S. Supreme Court decision that ruled it was up to the trial court to determine whether or not there was a privilege to withhold documents or information. On September 21, 1950, Judge Kirkpatrick ordered that the documents in question be given to him in privacy, and after his review of them, he would allow the plaintiffs to inspect and copy all of the documents <u>except</u> any part(s) which he determined to be privileged from discovery. This was the first time in the lawsuit that the government alluded to national security or state secrets.

It is important to pause and to discuss the meaning of 'state secrets'. It has been well settled in the common law (court rulings) for centuries that a government has the right to conceal information that constitutes 'state secrets', which include military information, matters necessary for defense, and information necessary for national security. I have no doubt that every American President has concealed or withheld, at his own discretion, what he deemed to be 'state secrets' regardless of any judicial ruling to the contrary. By doing so, a president usurps the proper role of the courts in overseeing the operations of the executive branch of the government, the very purpose of the checks and balances in our three part government, and in direct violation of the Constitution.

But unbeknownst to anyone involved in the lawsuit, and not disclosed to Judge Fitzpatrick, on September 14, 1950, just seven days before Judge Kirkpatrick's ruling, the Air Force reduced the security status of the requested records from 'secret' to 'restricted', which officially means they are available for official use only, or when disclosure should be limited for reasons of 'administrative privacy'. By downgrading their security status, the government implicitly acknowledged that the documents contained no 'state secrets'.

Still the government refused to produce the documents to Judge Kirkpatrick, prompting him to enter a default judgment against the government declaring that the government was negligent and therefore liable to the plaintiffs. The only matter yet to be determined was the amount of damages to be awarded to the plaintiffs. After a hearing on the matter, Judge Kirkpatrick ordered damages of $80,000. (now $622,972.) for Mrs. Palya and Mrs. Brauner, and $65,000. (now $506,165.) for Mrs. Reynolds. This was due to Mr. Reynolds' lower expected lifetime earnings. On February 20, 1951, he formally ordered that the government pay these awards to the plaintiffs.

Not surprisingly, the government appealed Judge Kirkpatrick's ruling. Along with other issues, it argued to the 3rd Circuit Court of Appeals that, most importantly, no judge could force the executive branch to hand over documents, and that the judiciary had no right to review Finletter's claim of privilege. It stated that "We believe that the determination of what documents should not be disclosed is necessarily within the discretion and distinctive knowledge of the executive branch". Months later, the Court of Appeals unanimously upheld Judge KirkPatrick's rulings and judgment for the plaintiffs. What bothered the Appeals Court the most was the assertion of unilateral executive power, free from judicial review, to decide what qualified as being 'secret'. After all, Kirkpatrick had not ordered public disclosure of the documents; only that they be given to him for private review.

Again, not surprisingly, the government petitioned the Supreme Court to review the decision of the appeals court. By a vote of 5-4, the Supreme Court agreed to review the case. On October 21, 1952, the attorneys gathered in the Supreme Court for their arguments. The government argued that by consenting to be sued (the Federal Tort Claims Act), it had not created any obligation upon itself to disclose information which various department heads declined to disclose. The logical extension of this argument, as pointed out by Biddle, was that department heads could refuse to disclose information about the routine operations of their department, but the government continued to vehemently argue that the courts had no jurisdiction to oversee the executive branch's decisions regarding disclosure. It argued that the right to disclose or not rested solely with the executive branch, and that courts could not even question the executive regarding the refusal to disclose. The courts must accept the executive's decision as final, binding, and not subject to review. Or so the government argued. Biddle argued that not only was it inherent in the Constitution that the judicial branch had the right, indeed, the duty of executive oversight, but that the plaintiffs had not requested any information which could possibly relate to military secrets, state secrets or national security. They sought only information on the individual plane itself, a plane which Russia had already duplicated to exacting detail, and the details of which were no longer an American secret. By a vote of 6-3, the Supreme Court reversed the Appeals Court and Judge Kirkpatrick. In a conciliatory attempt, Chief Justice Vinson advised the federal courts that although they could not completely abdicate their control over the evidence to the "caprice of executive officers", if the government can convince the court that "a reasonable danger" to national security exists, the courts should not insist upon examining the documents, even privately. But the Supreme Court did not dismiss the case; it sent it back to Judge Kirkpatrick for trial.

So Biddle was back to square one, except that now the Supreme Court had denied him access to crucial evidence. He took the depositions of the three surviving crew members, all of whom made it clear that the secret equipment on board had nothing to do with the accident, and that the secret equipment had not even been activated. A few months later, the plaintiffs and the government settled the claim for 75% of the original claim. Biddle received a contingency fee of 20%. The plaintiffs agreed to dismiss the case. So the three widows had money that enabled their lives to be far more comfortable, and the government had its newly cemented state secrets privilege. The B-29 accident report stayed out of public view. In 1954, the Air Force retired the entire B-29 fleet due to its poor safety record. But, in Biddle's view, the case was a travesty because of the loss of authority that the Supreme Court had forfeited to the executive branch. The three party government envisioned by our founding fathers was no more. The year was 1953.

There was little immediate effect in the courts as a result of the Reynolds doctrine. In the first twenty years after the ruling, the state secrets issue arose only in a handful of cases. Some resulted in upholding the government's claim; others denied it. But in 1974, the pace quickly escalated. First, Richard Nixon sought to invoke 'executive privilege' regarding recordings and documents related to the Watergate scandal. His claim was denied by the Supreme Court because he claimed only an executive privilege of confidentiality rather than a privilege based upon state secrets. This inspired future presidents and agencies to universally cite the state secrets privilege because the Supreme Court had drawn the line in the sand: A 'state secrets' claim granted the president an absolute privilege of secrecy. In 1971, in the Pentagon Papers case, Erwin Griswold, representing the government, stood before the Supreme Court and argued that publication of the Pentagon Papers posed "a grave and immediate danger to the security of the United States". But in 1989, he had completely reversed his opinion by stating that:

> *"I have never seen any trace of a threat to the national security from the publication of the Pentagon Papers. Indeed, I have never seen it even suggested that there was an actual threat......."*

> *It quickly becomes apparent to any person who has considerable experience with classified material that there is a massive overclassification and that the principal concern of the classifiers is not with national security but rather with governmental embarrassment of one sort or another."*

Over time, it became clear that cases involving claims of state secrets were falling into two categories: those where judges dismissed cases because a successful governmental claim of the privilege prevented plaintiffs from obtaining needed evidence, and those where courts refused to hear the matter at all because a trial might reveal 'sensitive' information. Clearly, the government held all the cards, and Department of Justice lawyers invoked the state secrets privilege promiscuously. As recently as August, 2011, the Justice Department has refused to release the legal memos which the Bush 43 administration used to justify its warrant-less surveillance programs. In June, 2012, Barack Obama invoked executive privilege to prevent Congress from seeing 'Fast and Furious' documents that Attorney General Eric Holder refused to disclose. It was an insult and a mockery to Congress. (Note: a federal court has recently rejected that DOJ claim because the DOJ had already released much of the information. The court did not reject the state secrets theory in and of itself). And in November, 2011, the Justice Department announced that it was dropping a proposal that would have allowed law-enforcement agencies to tell people making Freedom of Information Act requests that the government has no records on a subject, when it actually does. Why the Department of Justice ever admitted that it was considering such a policy is beyond comprehension.

Back to the Banshee Project: In 1996, the Clinton administration declassified all of the Banshee crash records. There is nothing in them about any military research. They involved only the plane's mechanical failure. I repeat: All of the government's claims had been lies.

By claiming that there were military secrets, the government had lied to all three levels of the federal judiciary, including the Supreme Court. The two sworn affidavits, supplied by Secretary of the Air Force Thomas Finletter and Judge Advocate General Reginald Harmon, were false. They lied; they committed perjury, in an effort to cover up the Air Force's negligence and liability. Their affidavits were a part of the written record provided to the Supreme Court, and on which the Court decided the case in favor of the government's claim of state secrets privilege. In the entire matter, the government and many of its employees had simply engaged in a cover up. Attorney Biddle would have been delighted to have discovered that more than fifty years earlier.

So, the families wondered, what to do to bring closure and honesty to the entire matter? Charles Biddle's law firm, Drinker Biddle & Reath, was asked to take up the old case again not only to rectify the fraud perpetrated by the government, but also in honor of Charles Biddle's tireless efforts. After much investigation, and with the encouragement of the firm's litigation head, Wilson Brown, the firm agreed to accept the matter, again on a contingency fee basis. But the legal challenges were immense. How do you convince the Supreme Court, whose focus is on finality and closure, to reopen a case that was concluded in the 1950's? And what do you ask the Court to do in behalf of the original widows and their heirs? A junior associate in the firm, Jeff Almeida, fascinated by the challenge and uniqueness of the case, asked to participate.

And so began extensive research into all of the old court records, including the entire record in the Supreme Court's archives, the accident report, the records of the U. S. District Court and the Court of Appeals, legal research into the issue, and more perplexing, how to get the Supreme Court to hear the matter. That was no easy task. The fraud had not been successful on Judge Kirkpatrick, nor had it been successful before Judge Albert Maris, who wrote the opinion for the Appeals Court. The fraud had been successful only upon the Supreme Court, and so that was the only forum in which the fraud could be corrected. But again, how? After substantial research, including extensive research in Black's Law Dictionary, the bible of the legal profession, Brown discovered the existence of an ancient writ (or request) called the Writ of Coram Nobis, which was a rare plea for the Court to rectify a mistake of fact made before it. They did not ask for a change in the Reynolds doctrine. That would have been rejected out of hand. Instead, they asked that the Court set aside the settlement agreement and reinstate the default judgment entered by Judge Kirkpatrick and to compensate the plaintiffs for the full amount of the judgment, adjusted for the inflated cost of money and interest.

On February 26, 2003, the firm delivered a box full of Coram Nobis petitions to the security guards at the Supreme Court entrance, and by midday, they were in the Clerk's office. A junior assistant in the Supreme Court, charged with examining all new filings for compliance with the rules, and having never heard of Coram Nobis, returned the petitions to the law firm two days later. After three discussions with Jeff Almeida, the clerk agreed to accept the petitions, and the firm redelivered the box of petitions. The media's interest began and evolved into a frenzy. Even the White House requested a copy. After 9/11, during the Bush 43 administration, a proposal was even made to counter Clinton's declassification order and reclassify as confidential those documents that had already been made public!

It appeared that the Court had granted the motion to accept the petition when it asked Solicitor General Ted Olson if he wanted to file a brief. He did, and made all of the same tired and old arguments of the government. And astonishingly, he claimed that the two false affidavits did not constitute a fraud upon the Court, and that in fact, they were truthful.

On June 23, 2003, the Supreme Court delivered a one sentence ruling: "The motion for leave to file a petition for a writ of error coram nobis is denied."

It was over. Although, with the full support of his law firm, Wilson Brown made another attempt to reopen the matter, it was denied at all three levels of the judiciary, with the Supreme Court denying a petition for writ of certiorari. The real legacy of the entire affair was that lawyers, legal scholars, even Congressmen, began to question the tragic and unwavering deference of the legal system to the executive branch - the president. Our government, which for so long had endured with three separate and co-equal branches, was no more.

ABOUT THE AUTHOR

I grew up in the Midwest of the 1950's and 60's. Ours was a traditional family with a hardworking father and a mother, an RN, who chose to be a stay at home Mom. My childhood influences were family, community, and our Methodist church, in which we were quite active. I give my elementary school teachers huge credit for instilling in me an excellent early education and a life-long interest in reading. In early adulthood, I attended college and law school in New England, where I practiced law, served as an elected official, and built a family of my own. The latter part of my career was in the Southwest where the 'dry heat' of the desert helped one of my children recover from a chronic illness. My own health led to my early retirement from lawyering.

With my children now grown and my grandchildren growing, and finally having found and married my soulmate, I found the time to put my thoughts and opinions down on paper. This book is the result.

AFTERWORD

It's time for me to shut up. The last words of this book come from one of the 20th century's greatest orators and Presidents, Ronald Reagan.

In his farewell speech from the White House, given on January 11, 1989, he said that there is *"a great tradition of warnings in presidential farewells, and I've got one that's been on my mind for some time"*. He spoke of a *"new patriotism"* but warned that *"it won't count for much and it won't last unless it's grounded in thoughtfulness and knowledge"*.

"An informed patriotism is what we want. And are we doing a good enough job teaching our children what America is and what she represents in the long history of the world? …… We've got to teach history based not on what's in fashion but what's important …. If we forget what we did, we won't know who we are. I'm warning of an eradication of the American memory that could result, ultimately, in an erosion of the American spirit. Let's start with some basics: more attention to American history and a greater emphasis on civic ritual. And let me offer lesson number one about America: all great change in America begins at the dinner table. So, tomorrow night in the kitchen I hope the talking begins. And children, if your parents haven't been teaching you what it means to be an American, let 'em know and nail 'em on it. That would be a very American thing to do."

President Ronald Reagan

THE BEST TRUE LAWYER STORY OF ALL TIME

This took place in Charlotte, North Carolina. A lawyer purchased a box of very rare and expensive cigars, then insured them against, among other things, fire.

Within a month, having smoked his entire stockpile of these cigars, the lawyer filed a claim against the insurance company. In his claim, the lawyer stated the cigars were lost 'in a series of small fires'. The insurance company refused to pay, citing the obvious reason that the man had consumed the cigars in the normal fashion.

The lawyer sued – and WON! (stay with me here) Delivering the ruling, the judge agreed with the insurance company that the claim was frivolous. The judge stated, nevertheless, that the lawyer held a policy from the company in which it had warranted that the cigars were insurable and also guaranteed that it would insure them against fire, without defining what is considered to be unacceptable 'fire', so it was obligated to pay the claim.

Rather than endure the lengthy and costly appeals process, the insurance company accepted the ruling and paid the lawyer $15,000.00 for his loss of cigars that perished in the series of 'small fires'.

NOW IT GETS REALLY GOOD!!!

After the lawyer cashed the check, the insurance company had him charged and arrested on 24 counts of ARSON! With his own insurance claim and testimony from the previous case being used against him, the lawyer was convicted of intentionally burning his insured property and was sentenced to 24 months in jail and a $24,000.00 fine.

I told you it was the best one.

ACKNOWLEDGMENTS AND CREDITS

Kathy Dokken, my wife and soulmate, whose love and support enrich me.

Tom Nolan, whose reviews and critiques were as important as his friendship.

John Phillips, Tom's brother in law and a retired lawyer, who reviewed the book with a lawyerly eye and pronounced it good

Bob Zohlmann, the best and most creative lawyer I have ever known.

All of my children, whose own lives and successes reward me.

Sandy Behar, a friend who stood behind me when I wondered if anyone else would again.

Herbert Grossman, who cleared my mind so that I could accept the challenge of writing this book.

My parents, Bob and Carol Clark, who encouraged me to become a lawyer, without which I could not have written this book.

Jack Skala, who taught me the true meaning of friendship many, many years ago.

RECOMMENDED READING

The research for this book came from personal experiences as a practicing lawyer and as an observer, discussions with lawyers, judges, and politicians that I trust, research, court records, published opinions (the common law), and verified media accounts. My opinions are a function of my experiences and studies. They continue to evolve. Some documents and books that I particularly recommend are below.

1. United States Constitution, particularly the first ten (10) Amendments and the Fourteenth (14) amendment.
2. Your own state's Constitution.
3. Any book by Gerry Spence. Of particular interest are <u>From Freedom To Slavery</u> and <u>The Making Of A Country Lawyer</u>.
4. Any book by Alan Dershowitz. Of particular interest is <u>Letters To A Young Lawyer</u>.
5. Black Mass – Dick Lehr and Gerard O'Neill
6. The Brothers Bulger – Howie Carr
7. The Art of Advocacy – Lloyd Paul Stryker
8. The 10 Big Lies About America – Michael Medved
9. Claim of Privilege – Barry Siegel

www.ingramcontent.com/pod-product-compliance
Lightning Source LLC
Chambersburg PA
CBHW030751180526
45163CB00003B/982